CONTENTS

FIX IT

How to Make Money
Rehabbing
REAL ESTATE
for **PROFIT**
Even in a Down Market

and FLIP IT

Revised and Expanded Edition

KATIE HAMILTON and GENE HAMILTON

New York   Chicago   San Francisco   Lisbon   London   Madrid   Mexico City
Milan   New Delhi   San Juan   Seoul   Singapore   Sydney   Toronto

The McGraw·Hill Companies

1 2 3 4 5 6 7 8 9 0 FGR/FGR 0 9 8

ISBN   978-0-07-154414-6
MHID 0-07-154414-3

This publication is designed to provide accurate and authoritative information in
regard to the subject matter covered. It is sold with the understanding that the publisher is not engaged in rendering legal, accounting, or other professional service.
If legal advice or other expert assistance is required, the services of a competent
professional person should be sought.

McGraw-Hill books are available at special quantity discounts to use as premiums
and sales promotions, or for use in corporate training programs. To contact a
representative please visit the Contact Us pages at www.mhprofessional.com.

This book is printed on acid-free paper.

CHAPTER 13 QUICK FIXES, CLEANUPS, AND
REPAIRS THAT MAKE YOU MONEY   145

INTRODUCTION

We were thrilled with the response to this book when it was first published in 2004 and our readers ventured into the real estate market to rehab their first house and sell it for a nice profit. Back then, buyers were standing in line, competing to pay top dollar for houses. The booming seller's market was fueled by easy credit and a frenzy to buy before prices went higher.

To say that things have changed is an understatement. Today it's a buyer's market, with more stringent requirements to qualify for a loan and backlogs of new and existing houses sitting on the market unsold. Unfortunately for some, a large percentage of that unsold inventory is investor-owned, with many properties having been financed by interest-only or adjustable-rate mortgages that have now reset to higher rates.

While the downturn may be difficult for some, the sluggish market in 2008 is ripe for rehabbing. More houses on the market translates into more opportunities for the investor. Our strategy is based on solid financials, not exotic loans, so the conditions are ideal. It doesn't rely on double-digit appreciation to make you money. Our game plan involves buying property at the right price and making improvements that increase its value, and a key factor in doing this is using professional estimating tools to plan the project and control costs. This book explains our investment strategy of finding a "good" house, improving it, and flipping it. We'll explain what we mean by "good" numbers, and we'll reveal the formula we use to determine whether there's a profit to be made.

Some investors define flipping as buying property and reselling it without taking possession. Our definition is buying a distressed or undervalued house, taking possession, making improvements that significantly raise its value, and then selling the house for a profit. Thus, our investment strategy is based on the timely turnover of property, not a fast flip. In some cases, after improving a house, we find that it has a greater value as a rental property, so we don't turn it over at all, but instead hold it for future earnings.

If you've watched any of the quasi-reality flipping property television programs, you'll agree that the drama and crises are caused by rookie investors making serious miscalculations of their budget. In this book you'll find tools and resources that the experts use to plan and manage an investment project to avoid making those mistakes. In addition, you'll find worksheets that help you evaluate a property and checklists to coordinate and supervise the job. We also explain how to use personal financial software to manage your real estate investments so that you maximize your profit.

When it comes to getting a job done, we've analyzed how much it costs for over 75 improvement projects. For each of them, you'll find current cost data that tell you how much it costs to do it yourself compared with what a contractor will charge.

We've been investing in houses since 1966, when we bought a two-bedroom brick duplex in much need of repair. We were schoolteachers by day and fledgling do-it-yourselfers by night, learning new skills (and making many mistakes) as we patched and painted and scraped and tiled. One house led to another, and we began writing magazine articles, books, and a newspaper column about home improvements. We went online and created housenet.com, the first home-improvement site on the Internet and AOL. We wrote about what we knew—the houses we had bought, improved, and sold or rented.

For years we've been meeting investors at home shows where we've been speakers, on book tours across the country, and in online chat rooms on the Internet. They're young, urban Gen Xers, first-time suburban homeowners, boomers, and empty nesters, all tackling fixer-uppers.

If you're ambitious and intrigued by the potential of rehabbing property, we hope that you'll find this book useful and that it will lead you to a profitable venture investing in real estate.

To help you get to work analyzing property instead of copying forms, we prepared a companion workbook and CD-Rom. They contain all the checklists, worksheets, and calculators in either Microsoft Word (.doc), Adobe Acrobat (.pdf), or Microsoft Excel (.xls) formats.

CHAPTER 1

BUY, IMPROVE, AND SELL OR RENT TO PROFIT

How has your 401(k) or IRA performed in the past couple of years? Probably pretty well, but not as well as your house. The first edition of this book came out in 2004, when the red-hot worldwide real estate market was in full bloom. Well, the U.S. market has cooled off, but there is still plenty of money to be made by improving property for resale or rental. In fact, our $16,000 investment in a small house we were renting and then sold a couple of years ago earned us a $90,000 net profit. And during the time we owned the property, we received a positive cash flow from rent.

Population growth and immigration will create a continual demand for housing, and historically, except for a few years during soft markets, the supply has almost never kept up with the demand. When we first got married, everyone we knew was looking for either an apartment to rent or a starter home to buy. We were both teaching school and had spare time on the weekends and in the summers to devote to improving what we bought, so investing in real estate fit our lifestyle. Later on, when our jobs changed and we did not have as much time to devote to fixing up properties, we worked out a rent-and-hold strategy.

Before you read further, you must realize that as soon as you purchase a property for resale and not for basic shelter, you are taking on risk. Nothing is certain except, as the old saying goes, "death and taxes." Purchasing a house to live in has a long horizon. No matter what the state of the economy or the real estate market, as long as you can make the mortgage and tax payments, you have a place to live, and it will appreciate in value over time. One of the risks of investing in property is that you must sell it if you are to realize a profit, and it's difficult to predict with any certainly what the market will be like when the property is ready to go on the market. But in a sluggish real estate market like the present one, you can take advantage of the downturn and find property that is more realistically priced. The crazy days and overhyped inflated prices have come down to earth, so investors can seize the opportunity to fix and resell, fix and live in, or rent and hold.

Creating Housing for the New Millennium

There were many opportunities to purchase properties when we started, and there still are today. About a third of owner-occupied homes are now at least 45 years old and an additional third are between 25 and 45 years old, meaning that they are ripe for repair and remodeling. While over 40 percent of the houses built before 1970 had less than two bathrooms, today a home builder wouldn't consider building a new house without two or more baths. However, the older housing stock is often located in very desirable, mature neighborhoods, and when it is brought up to modern standards, it can be more desirable than new housing.

We think that a lot of what's driving the home-improvement boom is the desire to change older houses to fit a new lifestyle. Buyers today want kitchens and bathrooms that fit their more casual way of life. Just look at the new houses that are being built today. They have larger, family-oriented kitchens and more bathrooms that are more elaborate. Older houses that lack these desirable features are passed over by buyers.

Today's time-strapped home buyers are looking for a house that they can move into and call their own without having to remodel and improve it. That's where the opportunity is for investors. Many older homes are run-down, and some of them come up short compared to other properties in the market. But if you buy them right, you can make money by improving them to meet buyers' expectations.

On top of that, there's a home-improvement industry that is devoted to making the big job of upgrading these homes easier than ever.

You've seen the growth of the do-it-yourself movement with the invasion of warehouse home centers and specialty home retailers wherever you live. Did you know that the expenditures on improving, maintaining, and repairing the nation's 119 million homes totaled $280 billion in 2005?

We've been doing this for many years—we've personally renovated 14 houses so far—and we've never seen as many investment opportunities as there are today. You, too, can profit by investing in the right property and making improvements that yield a high appreciation and sell for a profit. This isn't rocket science; it's based on knowing how much to pay for a property, what kind of improvements to make, and how to sell or rent it at a profit. That's what this book is all about.

You're reading this chapter, so you are obviously intrigued by the possibility of profiting by rehabbing a house. This book will help you develop an investment strategy to find, buy, and improve property with payoff potential and explain how to maximize that potential.

You might be a fully employed individual who wants to build an investment strategy based on your place of residence. Over the years, you can buy a house, live in and improve it, and then move up to a larger home—or just sell it and move someplace else. If you make the right improvements, you can pocket a hefty profit that is tax-free.

You might be a Gen Xer looking for a budget-priced house in an urban area or a suburban homeowner who sees the value of your home continue to rise, so you want to invest in another one down the street. You might be a boomer looking to rehab a second home in a beach town to sell or rent, or maybe tackle a fixer-upper in the country, where you want to retire. Whatever your situation, investing in real estate can work for you.

What about You as an Investor?

Your goal is to create a flexible investment strategy that works for you now and in the future as your life and your career evolve. We've thought about this for a long time, and we are convinced that it's all about your level of commitment of both time and money, and your temperament, talents, and energy. Let us explain.

Time

Do some soul-searching, or at least think about how much time you can reasonably devote to this venture. You might have to consult your significant other if you have one, or a potential partner. If you are time-challenged now, your best bet is to buy a house in a good location, live in it, and work on it when you can. Inflation and the improvements you make will raise the value of the property.

If you do have some time to spare, you're in a good position to fix it and flip it. You can get in as deep as you want. Do the work yourself, supervise it, or hire someone to do it all. You can make money in each situation.

Money

How much money do you have to invest? We have never used the no-money-down strategies, so you won't find information on them here. Investing requires some capital, and we will suggest ways to raise the money and secure financing. And you won't hear us promising that you can get rich quick in real estate, because we think it's hard work and takes time.

Personality

Now, about your temperament and talents. Let's be honest here. If you're high-strung and get stressed out when you're caught in traffic, you may have a difficult time rehabbing a house because there are many ups and downs that you cannot control. If your talents naturally include managing people and details, you are most likely to succeed. If you like working with your hands and are gifted with tools, this is right up your alley. But if you're not handy, don't worry; there is more than enough work on the strategy end to keep you busy.

How is your energy level connected to your real estate investment strategy? It's surprisingly simple. Rehabbing a house is a second job that takes considerable stamina, whether you're managing the work of others or doing it yourself. It's physical and emotional work that requires a high-energy person.

The Right Strategy for You

An important part of your investment strategy is whether you plan to improve a house to quickly sell the property, live in the house for a longer period of time while you improve it, or improve it and rent it. This, of course, depends on the condition of the property, the extent of the work required, and your time and resources. We'll walk you through the pros and cons of different strategies that have worked for us and suggest how they might best work for you.

Investing in a Fix-It Property

We consider rehabbing to be a second job because it has all the components of a business. It is a business for many investors who have over the years parlayed their profits into buying and selling more properties. You'll have to decide at what level you're comfortable, but we'll give you a foundation to build on. We'll help you decide your strategy and level of commitment.

To begin with, we'll help you investigate neighborhoods and housing markets where you want to invest. Then we'll explain how to evaluate property for its condition and payback potential. We'll describe the type of property that we call a "good" house, meaning that it's in the right location and is priced low enough to allow you to improve it and resell it at a profit. And we'll explain the formula we use to do the numbers.

Our philosophy of "flipping" a house does not involve buying it and reselling it without taking ownership. We use the term *flip it* loosely to mean purchasing a house, improving it, and then reselling it. This strategy will work if you can locate and buy a house below its true market value and then make improvements that increase its value by more than the cost of these improvements. An important piece of that puzzle is finding the right property and controlling costs while you are improving it. The faster you can turn over the property, the lower the holding costs. We see time clicking away every day we're working on a house, and this is a real incentive to complete the job and get in and get out in the shortest time possible. To help you get organized and stay focused on a project, use the worksheets in the book. They're a handy reference and overview that we find useful in staying on top of a job.

Where's the Money?

One of the first decisions you need to make is how much money you can afford and want to invest in real estate, keeping in mind that no investment is totally risk-free. A lot depends on the economy in general and the housing market in your area in particular, both of which are forces that you cannot control. We'll suggest how to determine your net worth and decide your debt comfort level and financing options that you can leverage.

Investing in real estate introduces you to a cast of financial and housing professionals—bankers, loan officers, appraisers and home inspectors, insurance agents—and all of them will require your attention. They will present you with requests for information and forms to fill out for processing, either in person or online. Approaching a lender for a mortgage on an investment property is somewhat different from approaching one for a mortgage on a home that you'll occupy, so we'll explain the differences between the types of loans and programs. We'll also give you some insight into what lenders look for when it comes to qualifying an investor.

Working with Real Estate Pros

We like working with real estate brokers for a whole lot of reasons, not the least of which is that they have access to the latest listings. A good real estate broker knows all the different neighborhoods in his or her area and has connections with banks, lenders, and, of course, buyers, all of which are vital to an investor. We'll share what we've learned about working with brokers and suggest how to find one that matches your expectations. Reading a property listing sheet might seem like a no-brainer, but there are red flags to look for, so we'll explain how to read between the lines. And even though it's not as up-to-the-minute as a real-life real estate agent who calls you about a house that was just listed, we'll discuss how we use the Internet in our search for property.

Evaluating a House for Its Potential

When you're walking through a house, take along a copy of the property profile we provide in Chapter 8. This is a detailed checklist to help you inspect and evaluate the potential of every house you investigate. We admit that it takes some imagination and experience to see through a neglected house that's dirty and distressed, but using the profile should help you see the Cinderella in a less-than-perfect house and focus on its potential.

As the number of houses you walk through increases, keeping track of which property needs a new roof and which one is on a busy street but is in pretty good shape gets hard, since they tend to blur together and it's difficult to recall the distinctions among them later. So use these profiles to analyze the potential of each property and then compare the profiles to determine which property will be the best candidate.

Improvements and What They Cost

We've been writing about home improvements for 25 years, and we have seen dramatic changes in the expectations of home buyers. While a dishwasher was considered a luxury in a moderately priced home 20 years ago, today it's a necessary appliance. And a laundry room? Forget about it. Back then, all washers and dryers were down in the dark old basement. Today a laundry room is a hot button on a home buyer's wish list.

We'll discuss what adds value to a house and what doesn't. We're keen on improving certain spaces in a house, like an attic, basement, and porch that are already under the roof. We suggest specifics about room height, the location of stairs, and the structure itself that are key to expansion possibilities.

To show you how much those improvements cost, we give the cost of all the improvements you're likely to make to a house. There are dollars-and-cents figures for painting, tiling, and roofing, all types of flooring, hanging everything from wallpaper to wallboard, and countless other jobs. That part of the book is an invaluable resource that you'll refer to time and again.

For those projects that we don't list, we show you how to use the same reliable resources that many of the contractors you may hire will use to bid your remodeling work. Armed with these resources, you can make accurate estimates of the cost of the improvements you plan to make. The more accurate the costs of your planned repairs and improvements are, the closer you will come to realizing your profit goals.

Contractors

You need to know about hiring contractors—how to find them and how much they cost—so you'll find our advice about working with the pros helpful. Because hiring labor is an important part of the equation, we look at a job and ask ourselves whether we should do the work or hire a pro. We always do the grunt work, the mindless tasks like removing wallpaper that require little in the way of tools and talents. We usually hire electricians and plumbers for rough-in work because many municipalities require that licensed professionals do this work. We usually have floors refinished by the pros and use installers for flooring materials. We'll explain all this later in the book.

Managing a Rehab

Whether you hire a contractor to do the work or do it yourself, someone has to be in charge. A rehab is like any other project with a timeline, and someone has to be in control. We explain different ways to approach management, and we suggest that you use the extensive checklist for managing a home rehab in Chapter 15, which you'll find very helpful. If nothing else, it's thorough. While it may be intimidating, we hope that you'll copy and refine it so that it's a useful tool for you.

Controlling costs is the secret to making a profit in any rehab project or running a rental property. We will introduce you to easy-to-use, inexpensive financial software to manage your projects.

Timelines

The last four chapters of the book are timelines of houses we've worked on. We think a timeline is the best way to give you some perspective on a work in progress on three different types of rehabs. The timeline in Chapter 18 follows a fast fix-up (less than 60 days) of a ranch house that needed basic repair and cosmetic work. In Chapter 19, the six-month timeline chronicles the expansion of a two-bedroom, one-bath Cape Cod into a four-bedroom, two-bathroom home. Chapter 20 records the challenges and rewards of a three-year plan of living in and restoring a historic home. And in Chapter 21, there's a timeline for a condo rehab that we recently completed.

We hope these timelines paint a realistic picture so you will have an idea of the process. Naturally, each house was different, and so was our commitment of time to them. Although different in scope and time, each of the houses turned out to be a very good investment.

CHAPTER 2

PERSONALITY TRAITS FOR A SUCCESSFUL REAL ESTATE INVESTOR

The many facets of investing in real estate make it a demanding yet rewarding challenge. Among the successful career renovators we know, there are some personality traits and skills that they all seem to possess. These personality traits and skills will see you through the ups and downs and uncertainty of finding and fixing property for a profit. There's no guarantee, but if you have most of these tendencies, we predict that you're well suited for the venture.

Orderly and Well Organized

It's one thing to work on a home project when you have unlimited time and resources, but it's quite another to work within a time limit and a budget. If you are a handy homeowner who likes nothing better than spending Saturday in the basement futzing around, you might think that this trait would be ideal for a rehabber. Actually, it isn't. Working on houses for resale or as rental property takes discipline, as you need to waste as little time as possible. Handy or not, someone who can break a project into phases, itemize the tools and materials required, and then make one shopping expedition to buy what's needed is better suited to rehabbing houses than is a free spirit. If you have the vision to see the overall scope of a project and can break it down into compartments, you'll take a systematic approach and get the job done.

Tenacious

Anyone in sales will tell you that the most difficult, but most important, part of any sales job is closing the deal. Completing the transaction or finishing the job is just as important in rehabbing houses. The attractive appeal of a new paint job is lost when the sparkling walls and ceiling contrast with the dirty old gray on the window trim and doors. A new laminate kitchen floor looks spectacular, but without the baseboard trim, it's a glaring distraction. Tenacity is a personality trait that will see you through the ups and downs of working on a deadline.

Decisive and Reactive

Are you comfortable making decisions? Not everyone is. For whatever reason, making decisions can be stressful, but it can't be avoided when you're renovating property. There are just too many decisions that have to be made—will the work on a house overimprove it for the neighborhood; should you repair or replace the bathroom fixtures; what's the best color to paint the shutters? The list of decisions that must be made when bringing a house up to market value can be staggering, and often there's no time to mull them over. When you're running behind schedule and your order for kitchen cabinets is delayed, can you reassess your options and decide on a different type of cabinet—that is available? As life teaches us, the best-laid plans don't always work out, and your ability to rethink your options and recover from curveballs is important. If you are resourceful and can react to unexpected issues that arise, you'll take rehabbing in stride.

Managerial

There are more Indians than chiefs because many people are good worker bees but are not comfortable delegating tasks to others. When you rehab a house, you'll be managing and coordinating the work of subcontractors, making appointments with inspectors, and possibly doing some of the work yourself, all of which take considerable coordination skills. This gives new meaning to the term *multitasking*. There's nothing more frustrating than watching drywallers sit on their hands while they wait for an electrician to finish installing outlet boxes, or having a crew of painters arrive and wait for the drywallers to finish sanding seams. Rehabbing a house involves parsing out work to a network of tradespeople, and one person has to manage and coordinate their efforts so that the work is completed in a sequential and logical order. Even if you're retired and working on a house on your own sweet time, you'll need management skills to schedule your workload and make sure that it jibes with the overall schedule.

Communication-Competent

Are you shy and unimposing? Those qualities are admirable, but not if you're trying to find a house with potential, improve it, and bring it to market. Asking questions, following up, and nailing down issues require ongoing face-to-face, telephone, and e-mail communication skills. That contact is essential to managing a house rehab project. Taking the initiative and making contact with real estate brokers, bankers, and service personnel are key competencies. For a landlord, it's equally important to find and keep a good tenant and make arrangements to maintain the property in good working order. That dialogue is key to keeping a rehab or rental project on the mark.

Capable of Confrontation

Some of us just aren't good at conflict. We shrink from challenging the work or competence of others because we're not comfortable in an adversarial position. The ability to confront issues and people is important, especially if you're dealing with workers or tenants. When the Dumpster you ordered isn't delivered at the expected time, your choices are to wait it out or to pick up the phone and confront the problem. If your first reaction is to call the company and ask about the delay, that initiative will help you. Opportunities for confrontation come in many forms, from no-show tradespeople or the all-powerful cable guy to potential tenants who are continually late with the rent. You'll have fewer sleepless nights if you develop the resilience to handle conflict and take confrontation in stride.

Curious and Adventurous

No, these aren't prerequisites for Outward Bound; these are personality traits that will see you through many projects in rehabbing a house. Your curiosity about the materials and mechanics of a house and your desire to understand how it works could save you a lot of money, not to mention time. When you have a broken garbage disposal, would you take it apart or call for a replacement? The adventurous and curious rehabber would disconnect its wires, unscrew the bracket, and take it apart to see how it works—and might even diagnose what's wrong with it. A broken window elicits questions about how the glass is held into the pane (with putty), not how to buy a whole new window. The kid who annoyed everyone by asking incessant questions about why things happened just might become a very wealthy rehabber.

Physically Durable

No, you don't have to be Iron Man, but rehabbing a house can be very physical work. Even if you hire a general contractor to manage the project, you will be working overtime to supervise and inspect the work of others. You may be staying up late working on spreadsheets or getting up early to inspect a new roof. The point is, you'll be working extra hours, and that takes its toll if you're not in good physical shape.

If you're doing some of the work yourself, your good health and stamina are even more important. The physical work and stress of manual labor is not for the weary.

Compromising

This trait is most crucial if you are doing some of the rehab work yourself and you tend toward being a perfectionist. It is easy to overimprove a property by not knowing when to stop. If you tend to go to extremes, you can easily invest more time in a rehab than will be appreciated. You may enjoy your high standard of workmanship, but don't expect someone else to pay for it. Certainly a tenant will appreciate the hours you spent removing all the old paint on the window, but there's little guarantee that that tenant will pay more to live there as a result. Shoddy workmanship is never a good investment, but try to adjust your high standards to the economic realities of real estate and find a middle ground.

Able to Laugh at Yourself and Your Situation

If you can laugh about the mistakes and miscalculations that you've made, there's a good chance that you can survive any situation that you get yourself into. The ability to laugh and not scream or cry is most important when you're living in a fixer-upper while it's being renovated. Can you see the humor in locking yourself in the bathroom or locking yourself out of the house? There's a good chance it will happen. How about noticing drywall dust on your granola? The idea that some people are aghast at dust on their furniture and cereal with a peculiar white haze should at least tickle your funny bone.

CHAPTER 3

OUR PERSONAL "FIX IT AND FLIP IT (OR HOLD)" STORY

To be honest, we really didn't have a formal strategy when we first started working on houses. We bought a small duplex that needed a lot of tender loving care and just started to do what had to be done. Katie's mother, a widow raising five kids, had invested in real estate over the years, and Katie's sister and cousins were in the real estate business, so houses and property values were talked about occasionally. Most of those discussions went right over our heads because we were busy teaching school at the time and didn't see ourselves as budding real estate tycoons.

After a few years of fixing up our duplex, we noticed a "For Sale" sign that had gone up down the street. It was in front of a two-bedroom unit, smaller than the three-bedroom unit we were living in, and in a sorry state because an elderly person had lived there for many years until she died. The estate wanted to sell the property quickly in "as-is" condition. Property was cheaper back then, but our paychecks were smaller. The down payment on the unit was about what we paid for our small car, $3,600.

We probably would not have jumped right into purchasing the property, except that we were very familiar with the duplexes and knew what had to be done because we had just finished our own renovation. We scraped together the down payment and started to work. Our move into real estate was more of a knee-jerk reaction to a lot of relatives reinforcing the idea that real estate was probably a good investment.

Once, we went to see Katie's uncle, who had done very well as a real estate developer, and she asked him for advice on real estate investing. He looked us straight in the eyes and in a deadpan voice said, "Buy low, sell high." There was a twinkle in the corner of his eye. So much for free advice, but actually you can't state the real estate game in any simpler terms.

Fixing and flipping property isn't brain surgery, but it does take a certain attitude and aptitude to develop an investment plan, and hard work to execute it. Many of our friends and relatives have questioned our nomadic lifestyle, and it certainly isn't for everyone. We learned this early on when our friends were moving from apartments to houses. We all got together to help with the moves, but soon we were three moves up on everyone else, and even a case of beer was not enough of an incentive to bring out the troops.

Even before we decided to go into real estate full-time, our first string of two duplexes and a couple of house renovations gave us a financial stepping-stone to change careers. But these houses were not fancy—we couldn't afford fancy property. In fact, one house we fixed up was close to Chicago's O'Hare Airport, and when the wind was just right, you could almost touch the planes as they came in for a landing. To make things more interesting, the railroad tracks were about a block away. We bought the house really cheap, but it had a fireplace and a pretty good layout. We lived there for a couple of years, fixed it up, and eventually put it on the market.

It took a little time to sell because of its location. One Sunday when a real estate agent was showing the house, the wind shifted to the north and the planes started to take off on "our" runway. Of course, as soon as the planes began to buzz the house, a 100-plus-car freight train began to rumble down the tracks. We can still remember the dutiful agent and the client lipreading as a 747 roared overhead and the train thundered on by. Surprisingly, we sold the house, and for almost full price.

Back to our first two duplexes—it was not until we had fixed up the second duplex to the point where it was in livable condition that we had to make some choices. We had two places to live, so which one should we move into? We decided to move into the smaller second unit and rent out the larger renovated unit, which we had upgraded with a new bathroom and a finished basement. We knew that we could get a good rent for it. Another factor influencing our decision was the tax advantage: if we decided to sell the unit we were living in, we could roll the profit into our next house.

Uncle Sam's Incentive

Even in the 1960s, the tax laws favored homeownership big-time. You could roll the profit from the sale of your primary home into lowering the cost basis on your next home, which allowed you to delay paying taxes on the sale. We figured that because we had bought the new smaller unit at such a bargain price, the potential gain that we could shelter when we sold it would be larger if we moved there. The larger duplex would also produce a larger cash flow. This was the beginning of our "fix-it-and-flip-it" strategy. But we never got to test this because we lived in the new unit until we got it fixed up, and then—you guessed it—we bought another house, moved, and rented the house we had just fixed up.

It did not take us long to figure out that the government incentives encouraging homeownership provided a tremendous business opportunity. The ability to leverage the purchase of real estate (especially single-family houses) and the tax benefits at its sale are the two fundamental reasons that investing in real estate can be so profitable. We go into this in more detail a bit later in the book, but simply stated, you can purchase something of value with little of your own money but get to keep the total amount of the fixed-up property's appreciation and much, if not all, of this profit can be tax free.

The tax laws are even more favorable today than they were when we started. Because a good portion of many Americans' wealth is in their house, the government lets a couple keep up to $500,000 of the profit from the house sale tax-free. There are, of course, some restrictions on this provision, and tax laws tend to change, so check the current tax law. But unless Congress changes the law—and that is doubtful—if you live in your primary residence for two years, you can claim the $250,000 personal exemption or $500,000 for a married couple. So in theory you could make a $500,000 tax-free profit on your house every third year. Depending on your tax bracket, this break makes the profit 10 percent to 30 percent more valuable than the sale of another property without this tax advantage.

For example, $15,000 allows us to purchase a property costing $150,000 or more, depending on the loan. If the property appreciates 15 percent, let's say to $172,500, we get to keep the increase on the entire $150,000 value of the property, not just on the down payment. So, the $22,500 profit is almost a 50 percent return on our $15,000 investment. Of course, there are other factors to consider, like the cost of improvements and taxes, but basically the ability to leverage real estate is what makes it so profitable.

Whatever your investment plan is, consider the great tax advantage that living in an investment house affords you. By carefully planning your move to the property in your portfolio that has the most potential for appreciation and establishing residence there, you can save a bundle.

Adjusting to the Ups and Downs of the Economy

During the three decades we have invested in real estate, the economy has had its ups and downs, and so has the appreciation of our investments. Through good times and bad, we have been able to adjust our approach to real estate investing to accommodate the market and develop a strategy. We started fixing up houses in the late 1960s, and the market was pretty stable until the 1973 downturn. The market then softened in the Chicago area, and we decided to stay put; we had renovated a house, sold it, and traded up, so we had a nice place to live and cash flow from our previous investments. No market lasts forever, so as the economy picked up in 1975, we decided to sell our house and move on.

About that time, we both felt the need to change careers, so at the end of the school year we sold our house and bought a house that we thought had great potential.

We took some of the profits from the sale and bought a sailboat. Instead of moving into our new "high-potential" home, we placed our stuff in the garage, rented the house, and left for a year's adventure on our sailboat.

We spent a year living on our boat on the East Coast and in the Bahamas and enjoyed it. At the same time, the market came back. When we returned, our house had appreciated almost 20 percent, something that we can't take credit for; to be honest, we would have been happy if the house had held its value. The rental income covered the mortgage and taxes, so we were in a holding pattern with a nice profit. It was not a bad place to be—owning property that was paying for itself while we enjoyed some time off.

Buy the Worst House in the Best Neighborhood

If we buy a house to live in and work on over a period of time, we now choose one that offers the most potential for appreciation by being in a prized or up-and-coming neighborhood. It might be an area of town that has a highly ranked school or a neighborhood known for its large lots and tree-lined streets. It's the kind of place where people want to live because of an ambiance and character that set it apart and make it special.

In those neighborhoods, we look for the orphan on the block, the neglected house that's waiting to be upgraded to match the other houses that have been transformed with additions and expansions. Ideally, the house is the smallest and least expensive on the block, so that with improvements its value can only go up and it can become a plum property for a buyer who wants to live in that particular neighborhood.

Of course, investing in real estate is not all peachy and positive. The return on an investment, no matter what it is, reflects the amount of risk that is associated with that investment. Purchasing and fixing up houses is no exception. The game is simple to understand: if you can't make the mortgage payments, the lender will come looking for its money, and the property will be sold to cover the loan. As long as you pay the mortgage, you get to keep the property. So the primary exposure you face is not being able to make the payments, which is the risk every homeowner faces. As our property portfolio grew, so did the need for ready cash to keep the loans current.

Weathering a Decline in Housing Prices

As in all investing, there is no reward if there is no risk. Since purchasing real estate with borrowed money allows you to control an asset that is worth much more than the initial down payment, the profit potential is enhanced. But—and this is a big but—leverage can also work in the opposite direction and enhance the potential loss.

For example, in a rising or steady market, as long as a property is maintained, its value is likely to either rise or remain unchanged. But in a falling market, the property's value may decline even if it is maintained. For example, to keep things simple, say a highly leveraged property is valued at $200,000 and a down payment was 5 percent, or $10,000. This means that the lender has a $190,000 loan backed by the value of the property. If the value of the property declines more than 5 percent, then the lender will come knocking on your door demanding additional monies to secure the loan. In a really bad market, the value of the property might decline 10 percent, meaning that the most you would be able to sell the property for might be $180,000. So to sell the property you must come up with an additional $10,000 to pay off the $190,000 mortgage plus closing costs. Remember, you paid $10,000 down plus closing costs at the purchase so you could be out of pocket almost $30,000. Ouch; that hurts.

One of the best aspects of our fix-it-and-flip-it strategy is that unless you overextend yourself, you can weather market downturns. A good example of this is the market we faced in the late 1970s. Inflation went through the roof, which was great for real estate, but interest rates followed and buyers ran for cover. The market dried up in a matter of months. Who would buy a house when mortgage rates were skyrocketing? The answer is simple: nobody.

At about the time the market collapsed, we had renovated two houses and had just put them up for sale. We had not planned on holding these properties, but our plan soon changed and we replaced the "For Sale" signs with "For Rent" signs. We had a few years' cushion on the five-year balloon interest-only loans on the houses, and the rent covered the holding costs. When we eventually sold the houses, we made a bit less than we had planned because the extra holding costs ate into the profit and we had to do minor fix-ups after renting. The point here is that if you don't overextend yourself, our strategy allows you to weather most market downturns by shifting from selling to renting.

Making the Most of Moving and Improving

Another key advantage of the fix-it-and-flip-it strategy is that you can get involved in the process as deeply as you want. We started as fully employed teachers working on houses in our off hours and during the summer months. We then decided to move into house renovation full-time and eventually moved back and forth through several career changes, but we never stopped investing in real estate.

During the cooler real estate markets, we began writing about home improvements as an offshoot of rehabbing. With every house we bought and improved, we learned new skills and had a fertile supply of how-to stories. Magazine articles led to writing books and a syndicated newspaper column called "Do It Yourself . . . Or Not?" The weekly column, syndicated by Tribune Media Services, has been running now for 20 years.

Fixing and flipping houses allows us to choose just how involved we want to be. Sometimes we work at it full-time, buying and selling several properties in a year; at other times we use the hold or rent part of our strategy to allow us the time to work on other projects. Our approach to real estate investing is flexible enough to fit just about any lifestyle.

Today's Investment Climate Is Ripe for Rehabbing

When we first started fixing up houses, the mortgage rates were above 6 percent. Today, some 30 years later, it's hard to believe that rates are substantially below that level. In the first edition of *Fix It and Flip It*, published in 2004, we included a quote from a then recent report, "The

State of the Nation's Housing: 2003," from Harvard University's Joint Center for Housing Studies. It suggested a strong decade ahead for housing despite the lackluster economy. The center's latest report for 2007 paints a slightly different picture of the U.S. market: "After setting records for home sales, single-family starts, and house price appreciation in 2005, housing markets abruptly reversed last year. In 2006, total home sales fell 10 percent, starts tumbled 13 percent, and nominal house price appreciation slowed to just a few percentage points." Suddenly it was inventories of unsold vacant homes that set records and homes in foreclosure that were making the news.

So we are in a real estate market that has turned from a seller's to a buyer's market. In the mid-portion of this decade, some parts of the country had more buyers than there were sellers, and buyers were forced to pay full price or bid against one another for the property. It looks as if the latter part of the decade may be a buyer's market, where more property is available for sale than there are buyers. Sellers may have to wait longer to find a buyer, and that buyer probably won't be willing to pay full price.

We have been able to purchase, improve, and rent or sell property for a profit in just about any market. It may be easier to sell in a hot market, but it's harder to find property at a reasonable price that allows for a profit. Since the market has cooled, there will be more opportunities to purchase property, but there will not be the built-in double-digit inflationary pressures pushing up property values. There is a good chance that the rental market will improve, since new housing purchases have slowed. We remain confident that there will always be a market for a good house. You may decide that you want to concentrate on a specific type of property, build a portfolio of rental units, or invest in commercial property. Whatever your goals are, single-family residential real estate is a good place to start. As we explained at the start of this chapter, what we do is not brain surgery, and the lessons we have learned are worth sharing. Our plan is not a get-rich-quick scheme but a commonsense approach that allows just about anyone to participate in one of the greatest investment opportunities available anywhere in the world.

There's another perk from rehabbing houses that we've enjoyed, and it comes when we drive by the houses that we've owned and improved.

We like seeing that the houses are being lived in and enjoyed by families. Some look exactly as they did when we left them; others have been expanded and improved further. All of the houses have stood the test of time. And that little house near O'Hare Airport with the railroad track that almost runs through it—it's still as cute as a button. On our last drive-by, the aluminum siding we installed still looked good, there was a well-used swing set in the backyard, and the smoke that was coming out of the fireplace chimney told us that the family living there enjoys the fireplace as much as we did.

CHAPTER 4

LIVING IN A FIXER-UPPER: IS IT WORTH IT? WHAT'S IT LIKE?

Is living "under construction" worth the hassles and inconveniences? Only you can decide, but it's always worked for us through various stages of our lives, whether we were a young married couple teaching school, self-employed writers and entrepreneurs, employees of a large corporation, or a couple phasing into semiretirement.

Our first properties were small, and we learned by doing, either tackling home-improvement projects ourselves or looking over the shoulder of the plumber or electrician that we hired. When we had stopped teaching and were working on houses full-time, our permanent residence was usually in the process of being renovated, and we usually had a project house under way. Yes, this could get very complicated and unsettling at times, but as long as we had a few rooms that were complete and livable, we seemed to take it in stride.

In retrospect, we were often more concerned about the condition and storage of our tools and equipment, which became considerable when we started working on houses full-time. A garage became a key feature when we looked at houses to occupy, because we needed a safe, dry storage space for the tools and gear we were accumulating.

Kids Are a Real Concern

Living with children in a house that is under construction is another issue completely. It can be daunting and even dangerous to have little ones scampering around unfinished floors and playing in less-than-ideal circumstances. And, of course, there are real dangers of lead poisoning and asbestos in an older house that is being remodeled.

The Environmental Protection Agency has a pamphlet called "Protect Your Family from Lead in Your Home" and others available through the National Lead Information Center (800-424-LEAD). The agency's Web site, www.epa.gov, includes information about lead, asbestos, and mold (see Chapter 8) in the home, where it may be found, and what should be done about it. If you're considering a major rehab and you have children, do some research before you make a decision.

All children and most adults appreciate structure in their lives, and the unpredictable nature of rehabbing can be very stressful. If rehabbing takes you from one house to another, consider the effects on kids of changing schools—this can be unsettling. Many families get around this by narrowing their scope of investment properties to houses within a particular school district so that their kids don't have to change schools.

A Second Job

We think of a house that we are living in and working on as a second job that costs us money in the short term, but in the long run generates a substantial profit. It provides a place for us to hang our hats (and store our tools), and at the same time requires either our time or our money or both. But if we choose the property wisely and improve it with care, our investment will pay off. That's true for a single owner or two married wage earners who have full-time jobs that can support the costs of improvements when they are required. If you're considering buying a house to renovate but are strapped for time, consider buying the house with a longer-term plan and letting the value of the property rise over time. When writing about home improvements led us to building an online business, we stayed where we were and turned all our time and energy to the business instead of completing the house and buying another one. We converted bedrooms to workstations and worked at home until we found an office, all the while letting the home slowly grow in value.

If the economy is strong, that's a strategy that works. But if the real estate market cools off as all markets eventually do and, during this time your job forces you to move, you're vulnerable—not a good position to be in. Experience has taught us that you're in control if you don't have to sell and can wait out adverse conditions so that you can take advantage of a seller's market that will eventually return.

Prioritizing Improvements with a Plan

The best approach to living in a fixer-upper is to create a twofold plan. Start with a long-range plan for completing the house to its ultimate condition, with a working estimate of the investment dollars you plan to spend on the house. That's the overall plan and budget to upgrade the property. We suggest methods and give you're the tools to make the necessary cost estimates and plans later in the book. You will also find specific plans and timelines in the last chapters of this book.

Make a short-term plan that's more immediate. It should include quick fixes and repairs that are needed to make the house safe. Take care of a faulty roof, plumbing, heating, and other essential elements of the house. Then make low-cost instant-gratification improvements that you can enjoy while you are living there. We always paint the rooms and refinish hardwood floors to create a clean, new living environment.

Sometimes the first improvements are not cosmetic—such as upgrades to the heating and cooling or electrical systems. Both are often required in houses without air-conditioning or enough outlets.

No matter what our ultimate decorating scheme is, we start with a coat of white paint on the walls and ceilings to freshen the look and give the property a nice clean smell. Paint the ceilings and walls the same color so that you won't have to make the time-consuming cut between the ceiling and wall colors. We add inexpensive miniblinds to the windows instead of investing in expensive window treatments. Other quick fixes can include repairing a wobbly railing on the back stairs, replacing the handle on a sliding patio door, adding a new mailbox, painting the front door—any improvements that are necessary to make the property more livable, functional, and attractive.

If an older house doesn't have a shower, which tops our priority list of creature comforts, we have a plumber run the water lines and valves for a new one in the tub. Then we throw up a shower curtain, but we leave the rest of the bathroom as is until we're ready to remodel it.

In one house, there was no storage space to speak of, but there was an unfinished attic, so before we did anything else, we built pull-down attic stairs to give us access to the space. We also had to reinforce the floor and put down some plywood decking. In many bedroom closets of older homes, we have replaced the traditional single shelf with shelving components that greatly increased the storage capacity. These inexpensive improvements increased the livability of a house, and we could enjoy them immediately.

We put off any improvements that change the floor plan of a house until we've lived there for a while because it's important to see how the space works. Moving a wall might seem like a good idea, but until you've lived in a space to see how it functions, it's difficult to consider all the choices you have. While it doesn't seem so at the time, there are advantages to living with a kitchen and understanding its shortcomings before tearing it apart. Only by living in a house can you see how the windows in a room open up the space to daylight or recognize the need to widen the window opening to a family room.

Coping Strategies for Daily Life in a Fixer-Upper

If you like to camp, you'll love living in a fixer-upper because sometimes you are reduced to that level of preparing food or using a tiny bathroom or dealing with other conditions that are temporarily out of your control. This isn't always the case, but it's better to expect a worst-case scenario than to imagine that rehabbing your kitchen won't really change your life. It will. Planning and preparation, of course, can make the situation bearable, but when you tear apart the center of your household, it's going to affect everyone until it's all put back together.

Don't be surprised when the ongoing activity of contractors and inspectors moving through your home makes some family members cranky. It can be very stressful. Decide on an area of the house or some rooms that will be off-limits to people who are not members of the family. Many people undergoing a rehab project need an oasis that's removed from the day-to-day commotion.

We should emphasize that everyone in a household is affected when your house is a work zone, including your pets. Don't be surprised if your favorite feline doesn't like the idea of change. And Fido just might not adjust well to the noise and confusion of a major rehab, let alone welcome workers inside. The only bright spot for our pets was their enjoyment of smelling, licking, and discovering new openings for windows and doors and following new heat ducts through attic floor joists.

We always had trouble finding Pete and Repete, our cats, when the second floor of one of our houses was under construction. They'd find clever ways to squirrel into floor cavities and hide behind wall partitions that kept us searching for them. Once, the only way to lure Pete out of a floor joist was with the Thanksgiving turkey. The smell was what got him. The point is that you're upsetting all the members of your household (not just the humans) when you change the structure of your house and your daily routines and lifestyle.

When a Kitchen Undergoes a Major Overhaul

- Pare down items in kitchen cabinets to the bare minimum.
- Make temporary countertops with sheets of plywood so that you have some work surfaces.
- Create a makeshift kitchen with a refrigerator on the back porch or in the basement. Set up a microwave and buy microwave entrées, eat out, or get carry-home meals. Use paper plates so that you have to wash only silverware and glasses.
- Set up an inexpensive metal cabinet to store essentials in the kitchen or near it.
- Keep a shop vacuum handy so that it's easy to clean up after workers (if they don't).

When a Bathroom Gets a Makeover

- If it's the only bathroom in the house, schedule the work carefully so that there's always a toilet that works and a shower for bathing.
- Double-check the materials (floor tile, fixtures, and so on) when they arrive to make sure that they are what was ordered.
- Make sure that there's always one electric outlet to power hair dryers, electric shavers, and so on.
- Coordinate family members' bathroom time and keep it to a minimum (well, try anyway).

Getting Used to an Open-Door Policy

- Be prepared for an ongoing series of workers and inspectors, and keep a log of the days and times of their visits. Also make note of what was discussed, determined, or agreed upon, along with any actions needed on your part.
- Keep a folder, basket, or other container for receipts for deliveries that come into the house. You can file them away in the proper place at a later date, but this eliminates the need to search for them at this point in the renovation.
- Designate one area—a garage is ideal—for storing all the materials that come into the house for a project. Open all materials when they arrive; check that the size, style, and number are correct; and note their condition.

Seeing the Positive Side of a Renovation

Don't get the idea that rehabbing has only a dark side. We wouldn't have done it for so long if it were that miserable. There are many bright sides to bohemian living. For one thing, you have an ongoing excuse to keep things simple, which is especially handy when you're entertaining. Rehabbing is also reason enough to lower your standards for a clean house. It's the perfect excuse, actually. In its place, however, keeping the stuff in the house orderly is much more important. On another plane, it helps you prioritize what's really important to you and your family. We found that the challenge of planning a project, completing it, and enjoying the results was very satisfying.

The relaxed lifestyle calls for taking advantage of the situation. For example, when we removed all the plaster walls in the second floor of one house and exposed the wall studs and framing, we used nails as clothes hangers. When we needed a place to hang a pair of jeans or sweats, we'd bang a heavy nail into the stud, and voilà—instant clothes hook. Nothing could be simpler. At the time we were writing a series about remodeling for the *Washington Post* home section, and we were amazed to hear from many readers who were embarked on the same rehabbing adventure.

We had friends who let their kids use the walls in one bedroom as a giant canvas because the walls were coming down to become part of a kitchen family room. They used markers, paint, and crayons, and it became a favorite game room for all the kids in the neighborhood.

We found living in a house under construction to be appealing and practical, but it's not for everyone. It was our idea of double-dipping: you have a place to live while you are working on improving the property. If you are contemplating this approach, we suggest that you go to a video store and rent the movie *The Money Pit*. It is a comedy, but the movie brings to light, in a glamorized and exaggerated form, some of the realities of living in a work zone. If you watch the video and everyone involved still buys into the idea, you're ready to move ahead!

CHAPTER 5

TAILORING A FIX-UP STRATEGY TO FIT YOUR LIFESTYLE

Rehabbing a house for resale or rental is nothing less than a second job, but there are ways to pull it off on flextime. This chapter is a reality check on the amount of time and resources the project requires. You have probably already heard the old saying, "Time is money." This cliché is certainly quoted by businesspeople, especially in the construction industry. Before you consider jumping head first into rehabbing a property, take the time to formulate a plan that you and your family can realistically fit into your lives. Any venture outside of your regular employment, including investing in real estate, will require changes in everyone's lifestyle.

Choosing a Strategy That Works for You

There are several approaches you can take to tackling this challenge. If your present job and family obligations allow you little extra time, your best plan may be to buy, improve, and rent a small property. If, on the other hand, you think you can carve out the time and energy from your existing lifestyle and focus them on a renovation, a quick-turnover strategy may work better for you. This is called creative thinking. If you are willing to put forth the effort, you can develop a strategy to purchase, rehab, and then sell or hold a property, whatever your situation.

Fast Return on Your Money

To most real estate professionals, the term *flip it* means buying and reselling a property without actually taking possession of it. Of course, you can't actually fix it if you technically flip it, so in the context of *Fix It and Flip It*, we use the term *flip it* loosely to mean purchasing a house, improving it, and then reselling it. We think it's going to be more difficult to just flip property now that the market has cooled down. In the last half of this decade, it is unlikely that we will see the type of double-digit property appreciation that we saw in the first half. Our strategy works if you can locate and purchase property below its true market value and then make improvements that increase the property value by more that they cost.

The key to making this strategy work is not only finding the right property, but also controlling your costs while you are improving it. So the faster you can turn over the property, the lower the holding costs will be. As long as you hold title to the property, the clock is ticking, and each tick increases the cost of taxes, insurance, interest, and utilities. For example, in winter, you will have to heat the property to keep the pipes from freezing, and in a large or older house, this can add up fast.

Of course, this holding cost should be figured into your renovation budget, but if you can get the project completed ahead of schedule, it's money in your pocket. And should the project drag on and on, the holding cost will take a big bite out of any projected profits.

To be successful at a quick turnover, you must be able to juggle the requirements to get the job done and control costs. You must carefully weigh the possible savings from doing some or most of the renovation work yourself rather than subcontracting it out. Many times professionals can complete the project faster, especially if you have other demands on your time. The fast-turnover strategy may also require additional working capital because the cost of property and its renovation will be compressed into a short time. Turning over a property quickly also allows you to take advantage of the current market conditions and not have to worry about what the real estate market will be like a couple of years down the pike.

Gimme Shelter: Renovate to Occupy

One of the greatest advantages of investing in real estate is that your investment can provide you with shelter while you improve it and wait for another good property to come on the market. In the mid-1960s, we purchased our first property, a run-down duplex in suburban Chicago. The unit was basically sound, but it needed lots of TLC. We worked at painting the interior, renovating the kitchen, installing carpeting, and transforming the basement into a family room while we lived in the unit. This took several years to complete.

At that time we both held full-time jobs, and we didn't have the time or want to make the time to devote to a fast turnover. Eventually another duplex in the same neighborhood came on the market, and we bought it; we found a tenant for our first unit, moved into the new building, and started all over. Our first property was producing a positive cash flow while we were working on the next.

Another advantage of this strategy is that you can get a better financing deal. Lenders require a much smaller down payment if you occupy the property, and this can reduce the amount of investment capital you require. Down payments of less than 5 percent are not uncommon for owner-occupied properties. And if you are living in the property when you sell it, you get a great tax break because it is your primary residence. This is especially true since the downturn in the real estate market and the tightening of credit make loans for investment property more difficult to secure.

Renovate to Rent

When you plan to rent out the property instead of occupying it yourself, of course the holding cost clock is still ticking before the property begins to earn a return. But because you plan to hold the property for a longer period of time, the holding cost is spread over that period.

After the appreciation in single-family property that we have seen over the last few years, it's more difficult to just buy a house, rent it, and produce a positive cash flow. Rents have not kept up with property values in most U.S. markets. But with the slowdown in new housing and the rising interest rates, many prospective buyers will be forced out of the housing market and into renting.

A rental strategy is a good fallback if the market changes while you are in the middle of a renovation. We discuss this further in Chapter 17, "Renting as a Fallback Strategy." In a nutshell, here's how this strategy worked for us. In the late 1970s, interest rates went up like a skyrocket, and the housing market came to a screeching halt just as we had a property ready to sell. It was obvious that the house would take a long while to sell, so we quickly found a tenant because the house was in move-in condition. For the next couple of years the rent covered our holding costs, and eventually the market came back. The house actually appreciated a bit, and we were able to sell it for more than our target selling price. In addition, since we had conventional financing, the rent paid off a small portion of the mortgage.

Looking at Choices: Adjusting Your Lifestyle to Rehabbing a House

Investing in real estate can be rewarding, both financially and emotionally. Breathing new life into a run-down house is rewarding in itself, and the satisfaction of having your efforts appreciated by a new buyer is very gratifying and can be profitable. But like many things in life, rehabbing a house, even a small one, will be close to a full-time job. Even if you plan to subcontract most of the actual construction, you or a partner will have to plan and supervise the project.

Before you look for your first property, make a basic decision about the time commitment and the size of the investment that you can make. Any of the strategies covered here can make you money; the idea is to take the approach that works best for you. And who knows, even with the best-laid plans, you may find yourself switching from one strategy to another as circumstances change.

To help you decide on an investment strategy, spend some time considering how it will change your life as you know it. That sounds a bit lofty, but your life will change, and so will your priorities. It's true that planning is half the fun, but in the property-renovation business, planning and contingency planning are everything. Here are some topics to consider as you create your overall investment strategy.

Job Considerations

We are assuming that most of you soon-to-be real estate tycoons are now employed doing something other than fixing and flipping houses. When we started working on our early properties, we were fully employed schoolteachers. This type of work was demanding and the school day was full, but we did not have long commutes and we had most evenings and weekends off. Our schedules allowed us to work on our first property for about 20 hours a week without killing ourselves. Sometimes we had to really press on into the night to get projects like the kitchen and bath completed because we needed them operational as soon as possible. We also had holidays and two months off during the summer, the ideal time for us to purchase a property. Sometimes we were fortunate enough to find a property that we could close on in June, work on like mad during the summer, and put back on the market in the fall. Sometimes we weren't. The "renovate to occupy" strategy worked for us because we had the luxury of free time and we had the experience from our early investments.

Make a careful assessment of your present job and how much spare time you can devote to a real estate project. It's important that your time estimates err on the conservative side because it's better to finish a project earlier than anticipated than later. But don't be discouraged if the timing of your first house rehab project isn't right on. Scheduling work is a fine art, and when you don't have any previous experience, it's difficult to plan far into the future. If you are a neophyte, as we were, you will most likely learn that your first estimates will need revising.

Retired and Ready to Work

Retired empty nesters are foraging the country for investment opportunities because they have the time, the money, and the skills to transform property. Many of these people are looking for a house project as a sort of part-time job; others want investment property as a bridge job before they retire. They are stiff competition for worker bees with busy family lives that are looking for the same thing.

A key advantage that retirees have over first-time working investors is their gray hair, which counts for wisdom when it comes to buying and selling houses. No kidding. Most people have bought and sold houses during their working years as their family and their income grew. Those years of owning and maintaining a house translate into well-heeled experience. Retirees make up a growing number of seasoned rehabbers who have either the hindsight and skills to manage the renovation of a house or the time to do some or all of the work.

Relationships

Probably more important than your job is assessing your family relationships. Even if you are single, relationships take time to maintain. Managing a renovation project is time-consuming, and doing the work yourself can be downright backbreaking. Little League, that weekly golf game, and most social events take time away from an investment property. We're not suggesting that you have to resign from the human race to fix and flip a house, but you have to be realistic about how you spend your time. For some investors, fixing and flipping a house is their full-time hobby.

If you share your time with a spouse or significant other, is he or she willing to give up that time while you spend your free time and weekends at an investment property? Is your partner willing to devote his or her own time to the project? If so, how much? At the risk of this sounding like marriage counseling, we've got to tell you that rehabbing a house can put a tremendous strain on a relationship. Years ago we wrote an article for *Home* magazine called "Coping with a Handyman Special," and we got an earful when we interviewed marriage counselors. The bottom line was that the issues of time and money were hot buttons when couples were arguing about a house they had bought without enough time and money to see them through the project. Talk it out, work it out, and nail down the time and money you're both willing to invest before jumping in.

Up-Front Time Commitment

One of the greatest challenges you will face in your real estate investment career is finding the right properties to buy and improve profitably. The operative word here is *profitably*. Unless you live in a very sparsely populated part of the country, there are literally dozens of properties available for sale that need work. Some offer opportunity, but many are not suitable for fixing and flipping.

Searching for property while you establish a network of real estate brokers takes time. This can be fun; just be aware that looking at and analyzing properties will soak up a lot of time before you find the right project. Then as you get one property ready for market, you should be on the lookout for another one. In fact, the search should never stop, even while you are up to your neck in a project.

Learn the Time-Allocation Dance

As we indicated at the beginning of this chapter, you must weigh your time against your money. But the equation is not as simple as that. Sometimes your time is worth more doing things other than painting or hanging wallboard, sometimes not. Be realistic about your skill set.

You may be a great salesperson or computer programmer and a downright lousy carpenter. That doesn't necessarily mean that you can't fix and flip property. It does mean that you are probably better off working a little overtime and using that extra cash to subcontract the carpentry. The point is, if you have a job that pays overtime or gives extra compensation for extra work, you could be better off working on a Saturday or during the evenings and farming out some of the rehab work instead of doing the work yourself.

However you decide to budget your time, your involvement in managing the project will be the most valuable. You've created a plan to purchase a property, made plans to improve it, and determined your budget—these are all management skills, key ingredients for an investor. But in your planning stages, consider that supervision of the work is costly when you hire someone to do it. If you have the skills to manage the work, you may have a hard time justifying paying a general contractor 10 to 15 percent to do so. On the other hand, until you get experience, professional management might better serve a large rehab involving extensive remodeling and possible structural changes. Until you establish a working relationship with reliable subcontractors, a general contractor may be able to get the work done faster and in some cases more cheaply. In Chapter 15, "Who Does the Work? Who Manages the Job?" we discuss this in greater detail.

CHAPTER 6

FINDING THE MONEY

It is our experience that investing in real estate requires some ready cash and decent credit. We do not give "get rich quick in real estate" seminars, and we have not used no-money-down techniques to purchase real estate. We do it the old-fashioned way—we earn it. Sorry to disappoint—if you're looking for a financial-freedom seminar, we can't offer any advice on making money without working for it. What fits our style of investing is developing solid relationships with commercial banks and savings and loan associations and using consumer credit carefully.

During the last hot real estate market, money was cheap and easy to come by. Many experts feel that the loose underwriting standards used by some lending institutions and the advent of no-doc or low-doc loans (those with very little documentation required) made over the Internet helped to fuel much of the speculation in the market. Tightening these standards will make money more expensive and harder to come by, and getting a mortgage will probably not be as easy as filling out a few online forms.

When we started investing, banks and savings and loans were much more conservative in their lending practices. Most of them required at least 20 percent of the cost of the property as a down payment. Many lenders were reluctant to even make loans on property that was not owner-occupied. Fortunately for us, we lived in our first couple of properties, so the financing was easier to acquire, but we still had to put 20 percent down.

What many investors say about banks is true: banks are more eager to lend you money when you don't need it than when you do. We certainly found this to be true. However, by working with several commercial banks and savings and loans on our first properties, we established a good track record, and the institutions soon began to look at us as valued customers.

Real Estate as an Investment

Like any business, buying property, improving it, and then selling or renting it requires working capital. How much working capital you need depends on your creativity and resourcefulness, as well as on the scope of your project. One of the first steps to take is to decide how much you can afford to invest and want to invest in real estate. No investing is totally risk-free, and that's true for investing in real estate. As with other forms of investing, the more risk you are willing to take, the higher the potential reward.

The ability to purchase a property, improve it, and sell it for a profit depends on market forces that, for the most part, are beyond your control. A property that seems like a sure thing in a hot market may not pan out six or eight months later if the market cools off. Real estate is also less liquid than many other investments; you have to sell the property, trade it, or refinance it to realize the gain. Can you afford to cover the costs of holding the property and wait out a down market?

On the other hand, real estate ownership gives you a tangible asset: a house to live in, a rental property, or a vacant lot. Given enough time, real estate has historically appreciated in value. The population is always growing, and people need shelter. Inflation and the restrictions on new construction in many communities put upward pressures on real estate values. But at any given point in this historic upward trend, values will fluctuate.

City neighborhoods go in and out of favor. Some of the worst were once the best and, given time, will probably become desirable again. We paid less than $16,000 for our first duplex and were happy to sell it five years later for more than $28,000. That's a pretty good return on our original $3,200 investment. Today, some 25 years later, it is selling for $185,000.

Timing is a large factor in real estate investing. In addition to asking yourself how much you can afford to invest, look at how long the money can be tied up. Depending on your strategy, your money could be tied up for a year or more on a fix-it-and-flip-it project or for several years in a renovate-to-rent or renovate-to-occupy scenario. Funds that will be needed in the near future, like those for your children's education, are best placed in a more liquid investment (unless the children are toddlers, so that there's time for property to appreciate).

Get Your Financial House in Order

Take the time to make an honest assessment of your net worth and determine how much hard cash you can commit to investing in real estate. Even if you are going to try a no-money-down strategy (you didn't hear it from us), the seller will want to know something about your financial condition. Be prepared to bare your financial soul to the lenders. To determine how much capital you have to invest in real estate, gather together your financial records and get things in order. (Everyone should do this once a year, whether they're investing or not.)

You get an A+ if all you have to do is go to your personal computer and ask Quicken or Microsoft Money for a net worth report. If you have to plow through records and stacks of statements and commit your findings to paper, consider buying a financial-management software program. Lending officers appreciate receiving a nicely formatted financial report, and the presentation tells them that you have a handle on your affairs. Financial-management software is essential for keeping control of your expenses as you get into real estate investing. In Chapter 15, "Who Does the Work? Who Manages the Job?" we show you how to use software to manage your projects.

The low-tech way to determine your net worth is basic accounting. Take a piece of paper and draw a line down the center to form two columns. In the left-hand column, list the value of the assets you have. Include everything you can think of, such as savings accounts, insurance, cars, the market value of your house, investments, and retirement accounts such as IRAs and 401(k)s. In the right-hand column, list all your debts, including mortgages, credit cards, car loans, personal loans, and outstanding bills.

Subtract the right column from the left and you have a good idea of your net worth. You may be surprised at the figure—pleasantly surprised or disappointed; either way, it gives you a realistic picture of your financial condition at this point in time.

After you complete this exercise, it's the time to enter the information into personal finance software like Quicken, which uses what it calls "accounts" to store the information. The setup program that installs the software also creates a set of default accounts that include most of the account categories you need in order to pigeonhole your data. There are preset cash-flow accounts for assets like savings accounts and checking accounts, and there are credit accounts to track credit cards. Asset accounts track your home and your cars, and liability accounts track loans and lines of credit. The software will produce an up-to-date net worth report once the data are entered into the program.

What Lenders Look For

When we applied for our first mortgages, the local bank or savings and loan kept the loans it made on its books. It was careful about who it lent money to, and it tried to make sure that we had the means to pay it back. Today the lending situation is a bit different, since most lending institutions eventually package up their loans and sell them to third parties. The advantage to the bank is that after it sells the loan, it can relend that money. But in order to sell the loan, the loan's originator must be sure that it has all the proper paperwork in order, so this makes the application process a bit more involved. Since the market turn in 2006, low-doc and no-doc loans have shown a higher problem (default) rate than loans requiring full documentation that is carefully checked for accuracy. Be sure your application is accurate and complete. Here is an overview of what lenders evaluate as they decide whether to make the loan or not.

Credit Report

Your credit report shows the lender what kind of credit risk you are: how much you owe, whether you pay on time, and if you have had any bankruptcies, judgments, repossessions, or delinquent accounts. Your credit report is actually a credit history. It is created by data about you from many different sources. Companies that have granted you credit make regular reports about your accounts to the three main credit-reporting agencies. A good credit history allows the lender to offer you a larger loan at a better interest rate. On the other hand, a poor credit history means that the lender may offset the higher risk of lending money to you by reducing the loan-to-value ratio and raising the interest rate.

Getting Your Credit Report

Ordering your credit report once a year and knowing your credit-reporting rights are important steps to safeguarding your privacy. You can obtain a copy of your report by writing or calling one of the three credit reporting agencies (CRAs). Ordinarily the charge is less than $10 unless you live in Colorado, Georgia, Maryland, Massachusetts, New Jersey, or New York, where there is no charge.

It is important that you get an up-to-date copy of your report from all three companies at least once a year. There may be errors in the report, and you can have them corrected. This is also the best way to be sure that no one has hijacked your identity and taken out loans or opened credit card accounts in your name.

For a copy of your report write, call, or connect online with the CRAs:

Equifax, Inc.
P.O. Box 740241
Atlanta, GA 30374
(800) 685-1111
equifax.com

Experian
National Consumer Assistance
P.O. Box 2104
Allen, TX 75013-2104
(888) 397-3742
experian.com

Trans Union LLC
Consumer Disclosure Center
P.O. Box 1000
Chester, PA 19022
(800) 888-4213
transunion.com

To get a copy of your report, you will have to give the CRA the following information:

- Full name
- Social security number
- Driver's license information
- Current address and any other addresses within the past five years
- Date of birth
- Signature
- Home telephone number
- Employer

Credit Scoring
Along with your credit history, the three leading credit-reporting companies compile a credit score for each person. While the exact method of computing this score remains proprietary to each service, there are some general factors that are taken into consideration.

First of all, the agency looks at how long it has been tracking your credit history and whether you pay your bills on time. This goes for all types of bills, not just credit cards and mortgage payments. If you are constantly paying your household bills on a second notice, this will affect your credit score.

The agencies look at your outstanding debt. How much total debt do you have compared to the credit limits lenders have set? The closer your total debts are to the limit, the more this will negatively affect your score.

Other factors such as your occupation and how long you have been employed help contribute to the score. Also, the type and number of credit accounts are considered when deciding what credit score to assign to you.

Low credit scores (below 620) will affect the interest rate, the terms of the loan, and the loan amount. People with scores above 700 usually qualify for the best interest rates and loan terms.

Income and Home Equity

Your income is taken into account in qualifying you for a loan. Most lenders like to see a minimum of two years in the same job or the same type of work. The income used in determining your creditworthiness depends on the source. Salary or wages are always counted directly, while overtime or bonuses will be averaged for the past year or two. For self-employed borrowers, the net income is averaged for the past two years. Other income may or may not be included.

The income-to-debt ratio has two parts: your total housing expenses divided by your total income, and the total of all your debts divided by your total income. The more income you have relative to your debts, the lower the perceived risk to the lender. The percentage of equity relative to the value of your home is also an important factor for loan approval and the rate of interest.

Since the hot real estate market began to cool in 2006 and the subprime loan foreclosures increased, many lenders have tightened their credit standards. We think the very loose credit of the first half of the decade will probably be tightened in the second half. That's doesn't mean that you won't be able to get financing, but you will face a more demanding lender that will take a much closer look at your application.

Building Collateral

To increase the amount of money you have available to invest in real estate, take a look at your list of assets to see if any of them can be converted into cash. You may not have to sell a well-established art collection to convert it into cash; instead, you can use it as collateral to secure a loan. Besides taking money out of savings, here are some traditional methods you can use to generate cash.

Refinance

If you own a house and its value is substantially above the mortgage balance, you can free up the equity by refinancing. This is especially true when interest rates are low, but no matter where the interest rates happen to be, if you have equity in your house, you can apply for a new, larger mortgage.

For example, suppose you have an existing mortgage with a balance of $75,000. If your house has appreciated to a market value of $250,000, you can refinance it with a conventional 20 percent owner-occupied mortgage and free up $125,000. Basically, the bank will make a mortgage for 80 percent of the house's value. The new mortgage will be for $200,000, and from these funds the balance of the old mortgage is paid off, leaving you with $125,000. The length of your new mortgage can be increased from 20 to 30 years to keep down the size of the payments. However convenient this may be, remember that you are taking on debt that must be repaid and that you are investing this money in a venture that is not risk-free. Also in today's credit market you will need sufficient income to handle the larger loan.

Second Mortgage

Another method of freeing up equity in a house is to take out a second mortgage. Most lenders will make a second mortgage on a house even if you have little or no equity in the property. If you have good credit, you can get a loan for up to 125 percent of the house's value. The main advantage of a second mortgage is the low rate relative to other financing. But with the tightening of the credit markets and underwriting standards, these types of loans may be harder to get.

The most common type of second mortgage is a fixed-rate, simple-interest loan, and it does not change the terms of the current first mortgage. The interest portion of a second mortgage can be tax-deductible.

Home Equity Loan

A home equity loan makes particularly good sense if you already have a low interest rate on your first mortgage. Most lenders offer flexible loan guidelines that allow a home equity loan to be used to pay off debts, make home improvements, or some combination including personal cash out.

Many lenders do not require home equity for a new loan, and programs for up to 100 percent or more of the value of your house are available. Terms can range from 5 to 30 years. The tax savings can be substantial when compared to nondeductible debt. Check with your tax advisor for current details.

Home Equity Credit Line

A home equity credit line is a revolving credit line account secured by the equity in your home. This type of loan has a variable interest rate based on the prime rate. The loan can be active for a long period, typically 10 to 15 years. During this period, you have the option of making interest-only payments or regular amortized payments. At the end of the line of credit period, the existing balance may be converted to a standard loan.

The major difference between a home equity credit line and a home equity loan is that with a credit line, you withdraw funds only as needed. For example, your line of credit may be for $50,000, but if you need only $20,000 for a down payment on an investment property, you draw on the line of credit for only $20,000 and pay interest only on the actual amount you use.

Many lenders will extend a credit line for up to 100 percent of the value of your house. A home equity credit line is available for owner-occupied single-family homes, condominiums, and townhouses. Because an equity credit line is secured by your primary home, the interest may be tax-deductible.

Sell Your House and Downsize

Another way to realize the equity that has built up in your home is to sell it and purchase a less valuable property. The funds are tax-sheltered, and you will save the interest that you have to pay on borrowed funds. This method allows you to get investment capital without having to use your house as collateral. Any business venture has risk involved, including investing in real estate. Using this technique is a bit more expensive, since you have extra costs such as moving, but you free up money to invest that is not tied to debt on your house, so you are assured of a roof over your head as long as you pay your new mortgage.

Borrow Against Your Assets

Banks will make loans secured by other types of assets, such as cars, boats, jewelry, certificates of deposit (CDs), and collections. Of course, the lender must consider the asset valuable enough. In some cases the collateral can be used to secure a portion of a personal loan, allowing the lender to make a larger loan than it would based on your signature alone.

Personal Loan

People with good credit may be able to secure a personal loan without having to pledge assets as collateral. Unless the borrower has considerable personal wealth and a good relationship with the lender, however, few institutions will lend large sums of money secured by a signature only.

Family, friends, and business associates may be willing to make a personal loan, and this may be a good source for a small amount of money needed to put the finishing touches on a property. For example, if your equity line of credit is several thousand dollars short and a quick $5,000 loan from a relative will give you the capital to complete a house and get a "For Rent" sign on the front lawn, this may be the way to go.

Set Your Budget

Before we look at the different financing options available to you as a real estate investor, you need to decide the dollar amount that you can afford to invest and are comfortable risking. If you already have property, you have to decide how much you want to earmark for real estate.

Using debt to buy consumer goods such as a TV or a car produces no return because those items depreciate in value. But borrowing funds to purchase assets such as real estate that can increase in value is a technique that has been used for centuries and is the basis of many large fortunes. Debt allows you to leverage the funds you have in order to increase your return on investment.

An important point to remember in deciding on your debt comfort level is that debt, if used wisely, is good. One of the best aspects of real estate investing is that you can enter the business at any level where you feel comfortable. Our first properties were very modest duplexes that we lived in, so we were able to secure favorable financing. As of May 2007, the median price of existing homes (meaning that half cost more than this and half cost less) was $223,700. For example, if you could purchase a property for this amount using an owner-occupied 90 percent mortgage you would need less than $25,000 down payment. A modest renovation might call for $10,000 in repairs, so basically a budget of about $35,000 is needed.

As the cost of property goes up, the initial amount of capital needed to purchase and renovate it also rises. The main point to remember is that if you purchase the property right and make the correct improvements, your rate of return will be good for any level of investment. Starting small does not mean that you have to stay small.

Whatever amount you decide to invest, don't commit the total amount to a single project. Always reserve funds to cover unexpected expenditures. Renovating any house, and particularly an old one, holds some surprises; by maintaining a contingency fund, you will be sure to have the funds to cover the unexpected.

Use Other People's Money

When you decide how much you want to begin investing, the next step is to look at sources of additional financing to leverage that investment. Remember that the ability to use other sources of money to purchase real estate is one of this investment's most compelling aspects. Leverage is the ability to purchase a property with borrowed funds, and it increases the rate of return on the money you actually invest. For example, if you plan to live in a house, you can get a mortgage for 90 percent of its appraised value. Taking the median house price of $224,000, you will invest $22,400 and the bank will put up the other 90 percent. Ignoring expenses, if the property appreciates about 10 percent over the next three years, you will be able to sell it for $246,000 and realize $44,400 in cash from the sale after you pay off the $201,600 mortgage. The $44,400 difference represents almost a 200 percent return on your original $22,400 investment. If you had paid cash for the house, you would have made a $24,400 profit on a $224,000 investment—a nice 20 percent return but nowhere near the leveraged deal.

Of course, just as leverage works to increase your rate of return, it can also work to increase your losses. Should the value of the property decline 10 percent or more, you could find yourself in a situation where the sale of the property wouldn't generate enough cash to pay off the mortgage. Not only would you lose your initial $22,400 investment, but you would also owe the bank the difference between the mortgage balance and the sale price of the property. The down side of the example in the previous paragraph is a steep decline in the market. The bank has loaned you 90 percent of the house's value. If the house's value should fall more than 10 percent, the value of the house that is used as the bank's collateral is not covered. The bank may request that you put up more money to keep the value of its collateral the same. But this is unlikely as long as you are making the mortgage payments on time.

If the market declined further, you would be required to either invest more money or sell the house. In the case of a 20 percent decline, the house's value could go down by $44,800. You still owe the bank $201,600. If you sell the house for $179,200, you must come up with an additional $22,400 or more to cover the loan. That generates a 300 percent loss, or over $67,200. Leverage works both ways, and it really hurts when it unwinds like this. Just look at the big hurt some of the high-flying hedge funds have experienced. As the market slows and values decline many homeowners find themselves in this situation since they have loans for 100 percent of the appraised value of the property. Compounding this problem, many have adjustable rate mortgages (ARM) that will reset at a higher interest rate.

Even in that scenario, as long as you make the mortgage payments and have the capital to maintain the bank's collateral position, you don't have to sell the property. Markets move up and down, but historically real estate values in the United States have continued to rise over time. The ability to change investment strategies to reflect market conditions can lessen the risk that highly leveraged properties can present. Changing from a fix-it-and-flip-it strategy to a fix-it-and-rent-it or fix-it-and-occupy-it strategy could allow you to weather a potential downturn.

Financing Options

Securing financing is one of the most important aspects of real estate investing. If you do not have a source of borrowed money, the advantages of leveraging are lost. The statement that there are many financing options available to anyone with good credit and a decent employment record was true in 2004 when the first edition of *Fix It and Flip It* was published, but it's now 2008 and the credit market has drastically changed. Historically low interest rates, overanxious lenders, and a real estate market filled with speculation have come to a screeching halt. In the near term, credit will be harder to come by, but not impossible to secure.

You may be reading this book long after the meltdown of the real estate market during the second half of this decade. If so, do a little research: look back at newspaper articles or visit financial Web site archives and check out how each of the financing options described here fared. It's a bit early to tell now (September 2007), but it looks as if adjustable-rate loans (ARMs) will lead the parade of mortgages in default. As you read through the types of financing described here, picture yourself with each type of loan. In today's market, how would you pay it off?

We will begin with the least expensive (lowest-interest-rate) options and work down the list. Many of these types of loans may not be readily available since the credit crunch. The underwriting standards have also been tightened. The era of very loose, low-cost credit is over, at least for the next few years or until the credit markets recover.

Owner-Occupied Financing

As long as you initially plan to live in the property, you qualify for owner-occupied financing. With this type of financing, the lender expects you to move into the property. It's not unusual for people to move because their situations change, so most lenders honor mortgages as long as the payments are made.

Just how long you have to live in the house is a tricky question. Most lenders do not check on occupancy once the loan has closed; they rely on your trustworthiness. Moving in, working on the property, and then moving on in a year or so would probably not upset the apple cart. You do want to maintain a relationship with the lender, so if you are going to use owner-occupied financing to get a better interest rate and a lower down payment, plan to spend at least a year in the property before you move on and rent the property.

Fixed-Rate Loan

A conventional fixed-rate mortgage offers you a set rate and payments that do not change throughout the life of the loan. A conventional loan is paid off over a given number of years, usually 15, 20, or 30. A portion of each monthly payment goes toward the principal, and the rest is interest. As the loan is paid off the interest portion of the payment goes down and the principal payment goes up but the total payment stays the same. You will notice that the amount of the loan goes down very slowly during the first half of it term since most of the payment goes to interest. As the loan matures more and more of the payment goes to pay off the principal. Most lenders roll the cost of insurance and taxes into the monthly payment so if these payments go up so will the total mortgage payment even though the interest and principal payment stays the same.

Adjustable-Rate Loan

An adjustable-rate mortgage (ARM) has a fluctuating interest rate. In most ARMs, the interest rate is fixed for a certain number of years and then is allowed to move up or down in sync with current economic conditions. The flexible interest rate lowers the risk for the lender, and in exchange the lender offers a lower initial interest rate.

The three most important factors to consider when applying for an ARM are the adjustment period, the interest cap, and the index used to calculate the interest. The adjustment period has two parts: the length of time before the bank can adjust the rate, and after that period, how often the bank may adjust the rate.

The cap is the limit on individual and cumulative interest-rate adjustments. The cap has two parts; the first is the total amount by which the bank can raise the interest rate in any given period, and the second is the total amount by which the bank can raise the interest rate over the course of the loan. For example, an ARM could have a 3 percent step limit with a 6 percent total. This will prevent the bank from raising the interest more than 3 percent in any step and limit the total interest-rate increase to 6 percent. A 5.5 percent ARM could not rise above 11.5 percent or go up more than 3 percent at any step. But remember, the loan payments have the potential to double over the life of this type of loan which is something many investors fail to take into consideration. Easy credit may dry up like it has recently and refinancing this type of loan is proving difficult.

The rate of the ARM is usually tied to some index or the prime rate. It is usually expressed as the interest rate you will pay for the fixed period of the loan and then the index, plus some additional rate that the adjustable rate is calculated from. For example, the index may be the prime rate plus 3 percent. For the 5.5 percent ARM in the previous example, if the prime rate is 5 percent at the time of the first adjustment, the loan rate will be adjusted to 8 percent. If the prime rate were 6.5 percent, the loan would be adjusted to 8.5 percent because there is a cap of 3 percent per step.

Balloon Loans

A conventional fixed-rate mortgage with a term that is much shorter than the term on which the payments are based is called a balloon loan. For example, a mortgage that uses a payment schedule for a 30-year loan but has a due date of 3 years is a balloon loan. This type of loan allows the bank to lend money at a fixed lower rate because the duration of the loan is short.

We have found that this type of financing works well with a fix-it-and-flip-it strategy. The plan is to purchase and renovate the property and then sell it. The balloon loan can be structured to provide ample time for the renovation, but the short term gives the lending institution more security.

In addition to the lower monthly payment that a 30-year payment schedule gives, many lenders are willing to make this type of loan interest-only because the actual equity payments during the three-year balloon period are small. At the end of the balloon period, you must refinance the loan if the property has not been sold.

Low-Down-Payment Programs

Many lenders offer loans that require little, if any, down payment. This type of loan will allow you to get the most leverage when purchasing a property. Until the recent credit crunch works itself out many of the loans described below may be very difficult to secure.

5 Percent Down Conventional Loan
- Most lenders will make this type of loan if you have good credit and adequate income.
- All loans are fixed-rate loans.

3 Percent Down Conventional Loan
- Most lenders will make this type of loan if you have good credit and adequate income.
- All loans are fixed-rate loans.

No-Down-Payment Loans

These types of loans, designed for first-time home buyers, make it affordable to buy a home you can qualify for and live in.

103 Percent Loan to Value, Zero Down Plus
- Finance up to 100 percent of the purchase price.
- Closing costs may be financed up to an additional 3 percent.
- Good credit is required.

- These are usually available on 15- and 30-year fixed-rate programs.

80/20 (80 Percent First Mortgage Plus a 20 Percent Second Mortgage)

- No down payment is required.
- These are available on 15- and 30-year fixed-rate programs.

Investor Nonoccupied Financing

Getting financing for investment property to fix up or rent is more difficult than getting financing for owner-occupied property. Banks will usually not finance more than 75 percent of the appraised value of the property, and the property must be able to generate sufficient cash to repay the loan.

Land Contracts

Land contracts-of-sale have been used for decades as a way to transfer title to a property when the buyer does not have enough money to purchase the property outright. A land contract-of-sale is a purchase contract where the seller holds the deed until the full selling price is received. Terms of payment are agreed upon between the seller and the purchaser. When the purchaser has made full payment, the deed is transferred. This method can be used to purchase property with little or no money, but most sellers will require a credit check.

Investor Financing for Rental Property

Most banks will analyze the income-producing potential of a rental property rather than the equity you may have in the property. The lender is interested in knowing whether the income produced by the property will cover expenses and pay the mortgage. Lenders look at the debt-repayment ratio (net operating income/total annual debt burden). Let's say you are considering buying and renovating a property that will produce $1,000 a month rent. That translates into $12,000 in annual rent, less a $1,000 allowance for one month's rent if the unit is unoccupied and total expenses of $800. That comes out to a annual net operating income of $10,200.

Many lenders require at least a 1.2 debt-repayment ratio. A little bit of calculating shows that $10,200 divided by 1.2 gives you $8,500. This figure is the maximum debt load that this property can carry. Depending on the lender's specific requirements, most would lend you an amount that has an annual payment of less than $8,500. If the current rates are 7 percent for a 30-year fixed-rate loan, the lender will be willing to make a loan for up to $105,000.

The easiest way to calculate the size of the loan is to divide the debt load, $8,500, by 12 to get the monthly debt load of $708. Then go to the Internet and use one of the free mortgage calculators to find the size of a loan at 7 percent that produces a monthly payment of $708 or less. It may take a couple of tries—if the payment comes out far less than $708, then raise the loan amount; if it comes out more, lower the loan amount. You can also use the mortgage calculator in the Quicken computer software program, which will calculate the loan amount directly. Microsoft Money also has a mortgage calculator.

To make this calculation easier, we have included a fully functional Rental Loan Calculator in the companion workbook.

CHAPTER 7

FINDING PROPERTY

Most investors remember the excitement and anxiety of searching for their first property. This can be a time-consuming process, with questions leading to more questions and feelings of uncertainty. You know you want to buy a house, and you think you know where, but it all becomes fuzzy when you begin looking at listing sheets, reading For Sale by Owner advertisements, and walking through houses. Be patient and channel that uncertainty by probing for information. Just as in any start-up business or new job, you'll learn the process one step at a time.

Finding a "Good" House (Property)

The first concern in the fix-it-and-flip-it strategy is finding a "good" house—one that fits your budget, requires the appropriate amount of work for the time and money you plan to spend, and will command the resale price you desire.

Find Your Zone

Narrow your market by deciding on a neighborhood, and then learning everything you can about that neighborhood. Consider this target neighborhood as your work zone, and visit it frequently on foot, on a bicycle, and by car. Choose an area not far from where you live if you plan to work on your investment property yourself.

Walking or biking through an area gives you a close-to-home perspective; you can observe the people who live there, see the way they care for their homes, and take a good earthy look at housing up close and personal. Shop in the stores, eat in the local restaurants, frequent any local events, and get to know the neighborhood.

A drive through the neighborhood gives you a feel for traffic and a broader outlook on the area. To take the next step and look at property there, get connected with a good real estate agent to learn about current values and who lives there.

Your Agent, Your Ally

A typical way to meet an agent is to walk into his or her office, introduce yourself, and explain what you're looking for. There's nothing coy about it; this direct approach lets you shake the agent's hand and see if he or she can help. Another way to meet an agent is through a friend's referral. And many investors meet an agent at an open house when he or she is the listing agent of the property.

A good real estate agent knows the neighborhood and will give you insights into the market, show you property, and ultimately shepherd you through the process of buying and taking possession of the house. When you look at property with an agent, he or she can tell you about comparable sales (comps) to give you an idea of the current value of the property. If you are buying a house to rent it, the agent can tell you the rental history of a similar house and possibly find you a tenant.

A good agent makes it his or her business to know what's happening in a neighborhood that might affect the market. It might be a plan for a new road that will have an impact on the street or area, an expansion of the library, the closing of a school, or a crying need for rental property. Whatever is going on, a good agent has his or her finger on the pulse of the neighborhood. But like any salesperson, an agent emphasizes the positive and may not volunteer negative information.

There's no substitute for a live person in a live real estate office with firsthand information about a property and the key to the front door to get you inside for a showing. Agents are used to answering a lot of questions, so ask them. Is a building permit needed for a new roof in the town, and if so, how much does it cost and where do you get one? Are there restrictions on owning a pet in a condominium unit? Is there a covenant against parking a truck in a neighborhood? Is there a time restriction for rental homes in a vacation area? You won't know the answers unless you ask.

As you look for property and before you ask an agent to show you property, make sure that you fully understand your relationship with the agent. The three common types of relationship that a real estate firm and its agents can have with its buyers and sellers are to act as a seller's agent, a buyer's agent, or a dual agent.

When you hire a real estate firm to sell a property, the firm and its agents represent you as the seller, and the sales contract obligates them to look out for your best interests at all times. However, when you walk into a real estate office and ask to look at property, your relationship with the agent who shows you the property may not be so clear. If the real estate firm has the listing for the property, it will be representing the seller. In this case, the agent will show you the property and must disclose all information about the property but has no obligation to keep anything you say confidential; he or she represents the interests of the seller.

If you find a real estate agent that you like and plan to work with, take the time to clarify your relationship. The agent should be willing to work as a buyer's agent, in which case he or she represents your interests and can't divulge any confidential information that you may choose to reveal. For example, suppose you and the agent work up a strategy for a low-ball bid on a property, expecting a counteroffer. An agent who is acting as a buyer's agent can't divulge to the seller any information about your plan—for example, how much credit you have been preapproved for or the most you will be willing to spend on the property. An agent who is acting as a seller's agent would not ethically give out this information but may not be required to keep it confidential. Also understand how the agent will be compensated. Most state real estate boards or associations set standards for these relationships. If you have any questions, get answers to clear up any confusion.

As you work with an agent, you'll find that he or she can be a sounding board for ideas, not to mention having a wealth of information about the nuances of real estate investing. Because a real estate agent deals with banks and lending companies on a regular basis, he or she can have a wealth of information about getting financing. The agent might be able to tell you which bank offers the lowest lending rate, which will lend to investors, and what percentage down payment each bank requires.

At the selling end, a good agent knows the specifications that are required for a house to qualify for a federal or state mortgage-assistance program, so he or she can advise you of any special requirements, such as the amount of insulation that's needed. If you are targeting your property to sell to a first-time buyer, this information will guide you in selecting the materials to use when upgrading the property. Also, the agent will know if there are any first-time-home-buyer assistance programs sponsored by the state.

Many contractors will tell you that some of their best customers are real estate agents who manage property and supervise repairs or maintenance on property that they have listed. These agents know and hire tradespeople that they can trust to clean carpeting, paint walls, fix plumbing leaks, and clean gutters. For a first-time investor, having a real estate agent with a Rolodex full of reliable contractors is a good beginning.

When a seller lists a property with a real estate company, the listing agent represents the seller. The agency receives on average a 5 to 6 percent commission based on the selling price of the property. The commission is typically split between the listing agency and agent and the buyer's agent. Some agencies or agents are "buyer's brokers" who represent only the buyer and do not list property. There's more about services and arrangements among real estate professionals in Chapter 11, "Buying the Property."

To find an agent online, realtor.com, the site of the National Association of Realtors, is a good beginning point. All the real estate franchises have their own sites, with similar "find a home" search engines and mapping based on the name of the town or its zip code. Some of these are remax.com, era.com, coldwellbanker.com, prudential.com, and longandfoster.com. Portals like MSN's House & Home and Yahoo!'s Real Estate have similar features.

What You Bring to the Relationship

You'll get the most out of a relationship with a real estate agent if you have a clear idea of what type of property you want to buy, whether you plan to resell or rent the property, where you want to buy, and how much you can spend. With that information, an agent can fine-tune a search for property and help you focus on seeing listings that meet your criteria.

Not all agents are created equal. Some specialize (or want to) in high-end properties; some have little time for a budding investor. But a savvy agent knows that a real estate investor is a good long-term client. By teaming up with an investor, the agent gets a sale coming and going because investors use him or her on both sides of a transaction: first to find property, and then to list it when it's ready for resale.

Finding Property

Real estate sites on the Internet have millions of house listings across the country and can provide a useful overview of the housing market in particular areas. Just type the zip code in the search box and listings will appear, some with photos and virtual tours of the interior of the property. The sites offer links to finding property for sale and for rent, identify agents within that area, and provide maps that direct you to those agents. So for an overview the Internet gets high marks for slicing and dicing listing information for the prospective buyer.

Unfortunately, these sites don't always update the information on a daily basis. You may see a property online and link to the listing agent to make an appointment to see the property, only to be told that the house is under contract. In a slow market when houses aren't selling quickly, that's acceptable, but in a hot market, it's yesterday's news.

Many investors buy property in the country or in vacation areas with plans to improve the property and hold it for rental income before they retire there. The online real estate sites are a vehicle for screening a geographic region initially and comparing prices. For example, in an afternoon you can find the price difference between a two-bedroom, two-bath condo near the beach on the east and west coasts of Florida. You'll also find the rental costs and restrictions for different beach communities. The Internet is invaluable as a research tool to learn about an area and then make contact with an agent there.

If you know the address of a property and want to find out about the neighborhood, use a mapping service like mapquest.com. You enter a street address, city, and state, and the site provides a detailed map of its location. This can be a great way to prescreen property and discover whether a house is in a good neighborhood or in a less-than-desirable area like near railroad tracks, at the end of an airport runway, or in a commercial area. This information may help you rank prospective properties and spare you the time and effort of looking at properties you wouldn't consider.

One leg of our strategy is a rental fallback mode. Be sure to check out the rentability of the property. Much of this type of information can usually be found online. How close is the property to public transportation? Are there any restrictive ordinances in the county, town, or neighborhood that affect the property? For example, many communities have covenants that outlaw or restrict rentals. Use this information in your initial screening.

LESSONS LEARNED

If you're planning to relocate to a new area and you want to find an investment property, subscribe to the local newspaper or go to the paper's Web site to learn about local issues and read real estate ads. When you visit the area, stay at a bed and breakfast, as innkeepers are usually very amiable and willing to answer your questions about the area.

For Sale by Owner

Having a relationship with an agent does not prevent you from looking for property that is being sold by owner. You can canvass a neighborhood for signs and follow the classified ads in local newspapers and magazines for advertisements of houses for sale by their owner.

The site forsalebyowner.com is a searchable database of properties in North America. It is a partner of For Sale By Owner Publishing Network, which offers links to regional magazines with properties offered by owner.

Foreclosures

When a homeowner defaults on paying a mortgage to a bank, the legal procedure used by the bank is called a foreclosure. In this procedure, the lending institution takes possession of the property and forces its sale to pay off the outstanding money owed. Typically, an auction of the property is advertised in the Public Notices section of local newspapers, then the sale is conducted by a court or sheriff's office, with bidders (buyers) competing with other investors to buy the property. We've never bought a foreclosed property, so we can't speak from experience. While there are entire books written on this subject, the best advice we can offer is to first find a lawyer who is well versed in foreclosure proceedings to learn the benefits and problems associated with such a transaction. Bottom line: if the deal sounds too good to be true, it probably is.

CHAPTER 8

EVALUATING PROPERTY

If you've done your homework and have identified the housing market in which you want to invest, you're ready to start evaluating property. The walk-through, or looking at houses, is a lot like prospecting, and we suggest doing some paperwork before you do the footwork. Remember that you're looking for a house where you have an opportunity to improve it through cosmetic changes, system upgrades, expansion potential, or any combination thereof. Use the property listing sheet as the first step before touring the house. Then create your own property profiles to analyze and compare all the properties you are considering as an investment.

Listing Sheets: Vital Signs of a House

There is a tremendous amount of property information on a real estate listing sheet. At first glance it reads like a laundry list, but the more listing sheets you read and process, the more you can begin to dissect the information and get an idea of what to expect when you tour the property. Before visiting a property, spend time reading between the lines of a listing sheet and use it as a starting point to raise questions.

Real estate agents use the Multiple Listing Service to exchange listing information about properties electronically. Years ago, this information was kept on paper in binders or on note cards that were stored in shoeboxes and updated manually. While the earlier information was cryptic and often contained limited descriptions, today agents can retrieve listing information in the blink of an eye and the click of a mouse.

This information is the vital signs of a house—approximate square footage, architectural style, the year it was built, sizes and numbers of rooms, type of heating and cooling system, type of siding, condition of windows and roof. You will also find information on the school district in which it is located; which, if any, appliances are included; and, of course, asking price and yearly taxes.

In the "Remarks" section of a listing sheet, you'll find features that the listing agent wants to highlight, such as, "Immaculate throughout this darling cottage." Depending on the listing agent's writing skills, a listing sheet may exaggerate conditions with superlatives or provide no details at all. In the listing sheet in Figure 8.1, note the Remarks section that cautions agents showing the property and prospective buyers by stating:

Figure 8.1

"Needs a little TLC." That's a phrase like "needs a face-lift," "fixer-upper," or "handyman special" that often describes a property that's ripe for rehabbing.

Red Flags to Look for at the First Showing

The listing sheet is your first exposure to a property, but it's basically a fact sheet that's used as a sales tool. You won't find negative information on the sheet, so it's up to you to see the property and do some tire kicking.

Your first impression of a property is important, and your reaction will probably be similar to that of other prospective buyers. Your mission is to look beyond the property's present condition and visualize what it will look like after you have improved it. Some aspects of the property can be easily changed; there is no accounting for bad taste when it comes to decorations. Don't let a purple bedroom turn you off, since the color can easily be changed; however, replacing old and outdated tile will be more labor-intensive and expensive.

We worked on several houses where it seemed that rose beige carpet was the rage in the older homes we bought. But under the carpeting, the houses all had hardwood floors that we knew were easy to refinish and were a popular choice for home buyers.

Another property that we bought had been owned by an elderly man who had not been able to keep it up. We opened the oven and found charred chicken parts, and the refrigerator was loaded with spoiled food. While the appliances were in working order, they needed a complete takedown and cleaning—a tedious and time-consuming project, but not costly.

Always look for the potential of the property, but don't overlook aspects that can't be economically changed. Here are some trouble spots to be aware of.

Standing Water on the Lot

Standing water on the property can be a sign of poor drainage, which can be the cause of a wet basement or a settling or cracked foundation. Be sure to walk around the lot and note any damp, mossy areas and places where the grass does not grow. Some drainage problems are easy to fix, but if the lot seems damp or if you see standing water, take note to investigate further.

Grading

The location of the property and how it relates to the surrounding area is a concern. Drive around the block and notice whether the property is on flat land or at the top or bottom of a hill. Ideally, a house is high, not low, compared to neighboring properties. Rainwater should be channeled away from a house, not toward its basement.

Water and Moisture Damage

Rain, snow, and moisture can cause damage to several parts of a house. Telltale signs such as wood rotting in the soffits where there's no ventilation and moss growing on roof shingles or the siding on the north side of the house are a tip-off to look for other indications of water damage throughout the house, such as looking at roof rafters for signs of rotten sheeting or rafters.

Dampness can also promote the growth of mold and mildew, which mean more trouble. The EPA says that there is no practical way to eliminate all mold and mold spores in the indoor environment. The way to control indoor mold growth is to control moisture. The agency stresses that to prevent mold growth, you have to fix the source of the water problem. Its Web site, www.epa.gov, has useful information about basic cleanup methods for mold. And remember that all absorbent materials, such as carpeting and ceiling tiles, that become moldy may have to be replaced. Water damage can be prevented with proper maintenance, but if maintenance has been neglected over time, the damage can be expensive to repair. Any signs of neglect should cause you to take a second look.

Structural Problems

Major structural problems such as a cracked or settling foundation can be very expensive to fix. Unless you can get a firm estimate for the repair cost and use the amount to negotiate a lower purchase price, don't consider the property. Carefully explore the cause of large cracks in walls, especially in corners. Large horizontal cracks can be a tip-off to foundation movement, which is not a good thing.

Underground Tanks

Underground tanks of any type can become an environmental disaster if they have been leaking for years. Be sure to check the location of heating oil, propane, or gasoline tanks on the property. You do not want to discover when excavating the foundation for an addition that you have a large oil spill in the backyard.

Well and Septic Systems

If the property does not have public water and sewer connections, ask about the condition of its well and septic system. Septic field failure can produce wet areas and poor drainage that can indicate a problem. If the property is close to a town or municipality that has a sewer system, will the new owner (possibly you) be required to connect to the sewer system? If so, how much will it cost?

Factors Limiting Improvements

In addition to looking for defects in the property itself, make sure that you check out any restrictions that local laws may place on the property.

Easements

Many properties have easements, which grant third parties certain rights to access the property. For example, if there is a utility pole located at the back of the property without any apparent access to service it, a utility company may have an easement that will allow it to come onto the property to service the pole. In this particular case, the easement is probably not a big problem, but an easement across the back of the property allowing a sewer line to pass could prevent you from placing a garage or some other structure there, thus making the lot effectively smaller. In all cases, find out if there is any encumbrance on the property.

Building Codes and Zoning Ordinances

If you plan to build an addition onto the house, find out if the zoning ordinances allow it. All areas have local codes governing property use, lot size and coverage, and how close to the property lines a building can be constructed. If the lot is too small, any or all of these factors may rule out building an addition or adding a garage. Corner lots, while desirable, may present challenges for remodeling, since large setbacks from the street must be maintained on two sides of the lot. If you want to build a fence around the property, that's another issue to be raised. Zoning problems can often be worked out and exceptions applied for, but this takes time and increases expense. Unless you are experienced in dealing with zoning issues, stay clear of these problems on your first investment project.

Historic Districts

Property located inside a historic district can be a mixed blessing to the investor. Being in a historic district often carries a bit of prestige and can increase the value of the property; on the other hand, to change the exterior, you will have to deal with another layer of regulation, which requires time and can increase costs. In general, these local commissions are concerned with preserving the integrity of the outside of the house, which usually includes windows. You have to go before a local Historic District Committee and present your plan for the changes. For the most part, these committees are reasonable, and if you are flexible, you usually can come to some amicable agreement. However, this process can delay the project and will probably increase the cost, since these committees generally favor wood over vinyl for siding and windows.

If you are considering a property within a historic district, get a copy of the guidelines and study them before making any decisions.

Environmentally Sensitive Areas

Property located adjacent or close to lakes, rivers, streams, and wetlands is subject to a set of complicated environmental protection laws. Many existing houses near lakes and rivers were built before these regulations were on the books and have been grandfathered in. Adding onto and changing these properties may be difficult or impossible. Also, property situated in flood plains can be burdened with additional regulations and require that you purchase flood insurance.

Condominium Considerations

If you are considering investing in a condominium, townhouse, or co-op, here are several things to consider in addition to the physical location and condition of the property.

Location, location, location is the guiding rule for buying real estate, and it's a key consideration in the condo market. A smaller number of condos in a desirable area often means that buyers have fewer to choose from, so there's less competition.

When considering the purchase of an individual condo unit or townhouse, remember that you are buying not only the unit, but also a share of the responsibility for maintaining the common areas of the development. Therefore, thoroughly inspect not only the unit but also the common elements of the building and grounds. Is there a monthly fee that builds an escrow fund to cover the costs of repairing these areas, or are there payments on demand when the roof needs replacement or the sidewalks need paving?

Ask about restrictions. Can units be rented, and if so, for how long? What about pets and parking spaces? Are there restrictions on exterior decorations like the size of flowerpots on the patio? Can you park a pickup truck in the driveway or add an awning over the patio without going through an elaborate approval process? Don't assume anything, ask questions and get answers so that there are no surprises.

It is essential that you thoroughly read and understand the conditions laid out in a copy of the condo agreement and homeowners association agreement. These documents spell out any restrictions and what the maintenance fees cover. If you would like the option of renting the unit, check the association agreement to see if that is allowed. You may find that yearly or longer rentals are permitted, but short-term rentals are not allowed. Also be aware that the document may be amended at any time the homeowners association comes to an agreement about a change.

Make sure that the unit you are considering is up-to-date with all assessments and maintenance fee payments, and find out if there are any special assessments imposed on condo owners by the association. Once you purchase the unit, you are liable for any money owed to the association. There are no standard agreements in this situation, so have your lawyer look over any documents associated with the property.

How Long Will It Last?

Appliances have a useful life, but after a certain point it becomes more expensive to repair them than to replace the unit. Carefully note the condition of each appliance. Even if you plan a kitchen makeover, many times you can reuse the appliances. Refer to Table 8.1 to learn how long appliances last.

Table 8.1 Average Useful Life of Major Home Appliances

Appliance	Average Useful Life*
Dishwasher	9 years
Refrigerator	13 years
Electric range	13 years
Range hood	14 years
Gas range	15 years
Kitchen faucet	15 years
Kitchen cabinets	50 years
Trash compactor	14 years
Microwave	9 years
Disposer	12 years
Freezer	11 years
Tub shower	20 years
Medicine cabinet	20 years
Whirlpool tub	20–25 years
Clothes washer	10 years

Appliance	Average Useful Life*
Clothes dryer	13 years
Room air conditioner	10–15 years
Dehumidifier	11 years
Water heater	11 years
Tankless water heater	20 years
Laminated floors	15–25 years
Vinyl floors	50 years
Tile floors	75–100 years
Wood floors	Lifetime
Carpet	8–10 years
Garage door opener	10–15 years

Source: National Association of Home Builders, 2007.

*The age of an appliance when it is replaced because it cannot be repaired or costs too much to repair.

Inspecting 101: Make a Property Profile

A property profile is a detailed checklist that will help you inspect and evaluate the potential of every house you look at. Use it as you walk through the house. It takes some imagination and experience to see through a neglected house that's dirty and distressed. The profile should help you see the Cinderella in a less-than-perfect house and focus on its potential.

As you walk through a house, look at the layout and the floor plan. Is there an unfinished attic that's suitable for expansion? What's the condition of the walls, cabinets, floors, and appliances? What about the heating and cooling systems? The items on the checklist remind you to inspect all the elements of the house so that you can make an informed buying decision.

Use property profiles to weigh the pros and cons of several properties by making one for every house under consideration. As the number of houses you walk through increases, they tend to blur together, and it's difficult to recall the distinctions among them. Spread the profiles out on a table and use the information about each house to either eliminate it from consideration or raise it to the top of the pile. While these property profiles keep you straight and help you remember distinct features and trouble spots, they also provide a handy way to make notes and observations.

Use a clipboard or notebook for the property profile sheet, along with paper to make a sketch of the floor plan. Bring a pen, a measuring tape, and a pair of binoculars (to look at the roof and chimney) when you walk through the property. If permitted, bring a camera so that you'll have photographs or digital images of the house.

Using the Profile to Compare Properties

We all make different kinds of lists; some are short and cryptic, and others verge on being anal-retentive. Err on the side of being anal when you're touring a property that is a potential investment because the more you record on the profile, the more information you gather that will help you make the most enlightened decision whether to invest or not to invest.

There is some information on the listing sheet for the property, but it's wise to verify that this information is accurate. As a matter of fact, at the bottom of every listing sheet there is a disclaimer about accuracy. So it's in your best interest to confirm that the type and number of kitchen appliances is correct, that a washer and dryer are included, and that the third bedroom, although small, does indeed have a closet. You'll develop your own code for using the checklist. Circle the "red flags" or signs of neglect and concern when you see a rusty air conditioner or missing roof shingles. Better yet, take copious notes and comment on the condition with a short notation.

To make this easy, use a digital camera or the camera in your cell phone to document everything you see. It's a no-brainer that just about any digital camera will do, since these photos are not going to be works of art. Going digital will pay for the camera in no time, since there is no film cost. In addition, the pictures can be sorted and stored on your computer so that they are easy to find when you are reviewing the properties.

A digital voice recorder is a time saver that takes your notes and records your impressions and ideas as you evaluate a house. We tried using a conventional analog tape recorder, but we found that reviewing the tape took a long time. When scouting several properties, we'd have hours of tape to review, which was cumbersome and took far too much time.

However, a digital voice recorder and voice-to-text software like Dragon NaturallySpeaking (www.nuance.com) makes it easy. The software converts the recorded conversation into text that can be edited on your computer. These text files can be placed with the pictures for easy review later. The prices of digital recorders have dropped drastically and run from $100 to $200, depending on whether the recorder is bundled with software.

Make the checklist work for you and your style of observation. Figure 8.2 is an example of notations on a property profile. Copy or scan the property profile sheets (Figure 8.3), and customize them for the types of houses in your area. For example, if the houses have no basements, delete that category. Add items that are appropriate for the type of property you're considering for investment. Full-size copies of these profile sheets are included in the companion workbook in easily editable Word or Acrobat format.

Figure 8.2 Sample Property Profile Notes

INSPECTION ITEMS	NOTES
Living, Dining, Family Room	
Walls and ceilings	*ugly wallpaper, gotta go*
Built-ins or fireplace	*nice mantel*
Bathroom	
Tub/shower	*mildew in corners*
Toilet	*flushes slowly*
Lawn and Garden	
Back and side yard	*large tree stump to remove; nice garden beds, need weeding*

Figure 8.3 Property Profile

Address:

Date of inspection:

Agent:

INSPECTION ITEMS	NOTES

Exterior Entrance

Walkways, driveway, and stairs   _____

Lawn, plantings, and trees   _____

Doors and location   _____

Living, Dining, Family Rooms

Walls and ceilings   _____

Doors and windows   _____

Flooring   _____

Lighting fixtures   _____

Number of electric outlets   _____

Built-ins or fireplace   _____

Closet   _____

Other features   _____

Bathroom I

Walls and ceiling   _____

Doors and windows   _____

Flooring   _____

Lighting fixtures   _____

Number of GFCI electric outlets   _____

Cabinets   _____

Countertops   _____

Ventilation   _____

Tub/shower   _____

INSPECTION ITEMS	NOTES
Toilet	_____
Sink and faucet	_____
Closet	_____
Other features	_____

Bathroom 2

Walls and ceiling	_____
Doors and windows	_____
Flooring	_____
Lighting fixtures	_____
Number of GFCI electric outlets	_____
Cabinets	_____
Countertops	_____
Ventilation	_____
Tub/shower	_____
Toilet	_____
Sink and faucet	_____
Closet	_____
Other features	_____

Kitchen

Walls and ceilings	_____
Doors and windows	_____
Flooring	_____
Lighting fixtures	_____
Number of GFCI electric outlets	_____
Cabinets/islands	_____
Countertops	_____
Ventilation	_____

INSPECTION ITEMS	NOTES
Appliances and their power sources	_____
Range	_____
Refrigerator	_____
Dishwasher	_____
Disposal	_____
Sink and faucet	_____
Other features	_____

Bedroom 1

Walls and ceilings	_____
Doors and windows	_____
Flooring	_____
Lighting fixtures	_____
Number of electric outlets	_____
Built-ins or fireplace	_____
Closet	_____
Other features	_____

Bedroom 2

Walls and ceilings	_____
Doors and windows	_____
Flooring	_____
Lighting fixtures	_____
Number of electric outlets	_____
Built-ins or fireplace	_____
Closet	_____
Other features	_____

Bedroom 3

Walls and ceilings	_____
Doors and windows	_____

INSPECTION ITEMS	NOTES
Flooring	_____
Lighting fixtures	_____
Number of electric outlets	_____
Built-ins or fireplace	_____
Closet	_____
Other features	_____

Additional Room

Walls and ceilings	_____
Doors and windows	_____
Flooring	_____
Lighting fixtures	_____
Number of electric outlets	_____
Built-ins or fireplace	_____
Closet	_____
Other features	_____

Attic

Walls and framing	_____
Signs of water damage	_____
Unfinished (usable as storage)	_____
Thickness of insulation	_____
Height at peak	_____
Location of stairs	_____
Electricity and	_____
lighting	_____
Finished (living space)	_____
Walls and ceilings	_____
Doors and windows	_____
Flooring	_____

INSPECTION ITEMS	NOTES
Number of electric outlets	_____
Lighting fixtures	_____
Closet or storage	_____
Other features	_____

Basement

Walls and framing	_____
Signs of termite or pest damage	_____
Unfinished (usable as storage)	_____
High water mark sign on walls	_____
Height of lowest pipe or duct	_____
Location of stairs	_____
Location of exterior access	_____
Proximity to furnace	_____
Finished (living space)	_____
Walls and ceilings	_____
Doors and windows	_____
Flooring	_____
Number of electric outlets	_____
Lighting fixtures	_____
Closet or storage	_____
Other features	_____
Sump pump	_____
Ventilation	_____

Laundry or Utility Closet

Washtub	_____
Number of GFCI electric outlets	_____
Power source for washer/dryer	_____

INSPECTION ITEMS	NOTES
Washer/dryer units	_____
Other features	_____

Systems and Mechanics

Electrical panel	_____
Location	_____
Amperage and voltage rating	_____
Number of circuits	_____
Limited or expandable	_____
Heating system	_____
Air-conditioning system or window units	_____
Hot water heater	_____
Water-softening system	_____

Exterior of house

Doors and windows	_____
Storm doors and windows	_____
Siding	_____
Roof	_____
Tight, missing, or curling shingles	_____
Chimney	_____
Loose bricks or flashing	_____
Porches	_____
Screens	_____
Potential to enclose	_____
Decks	_____
Boards and fasteners	_____
Stairs and railing	_____

INSPECTION ITEMS	NOTES
Patio	
Drainage and gutters	
Tight-fitting gutters and downspouts	
Pooling water around foundation	
Foundation and crawl space	
Signs of termite or pest damage	
Wet or dry insulation	
Ventilation	

Garage and Outbuildings

Foundation and soundness of structure	
Condition of siding, doors, windows	
Signs of termite or pest damage	

Lawn and Garden

Fencing	
Location of posts	
Who owns the fence?	
Does it mark the property line?	
Lawn and landscaping	
Grass	
Walkways	
Shrubbery and plantings	
Trees	
Yard structures or obstacles	

CHAPTER 9

HOME IMPROVEMENT FROM AN INVESTOR'S PERSPECTIVE

The housing stock of the United States is old. There are 61 million houses that are more than 25 years old, and 24 million more that are between 16 and 25 years old. Most of these older houses were built to a different set of buyer expectations. Changes in family life and new technologies and building materials have made upgrading the aging housing stock big business. There are a lot of houses for real estate investors to improve and upgrade.

The underlying principle of *Fix It and Flip It* is that with careful planning, you can purchase property below market value, make improvements to it that increase its value by an amount well above the cost of the improvements, and then sell it for a profit. Any house that you may consider a candidate for investment does not exist in a vacuum. A particular type of property located in one neighborhood may represent a real opportunity, but that same type of property in a different location may not be such a hot prospect. There are several factors that determine the value of real estate, and each of these factors must be considered when sizing up a potential property.

Factors Influencing the Value of Property

After "buy low, sell high," the next most quoted real estate cliché is "location, location, location." Location certainly is important, but it's not the only factor that determines the value of a property. One of the challenges you face when looking at investment property is to assess not only the current value of the property, but also its potential value.

You want to buy property that is below its current market potential. A property is worth exactly what a buyer is prepared to pay for it—no more and no less. You are the buyer, so you set the value of the property when you purchase it. The question you have to answer—and this determines your profit potential—is, can the property be changed in some way to attract another buyer who will pay more for the property than the last buyer (that's you)?

Let's take a look at all of the factors that influence the value of a property.

Location and Market

When talking about location, it's helpful to think of those animated shots you see on TV that start with a picture of the world and then continually zoom in until they show a scene of a particular part of a city or town. Taken from that perspective, location can have several nuances.

National Market

The national economy in general has an effect on real estate. National events like terrorism, war, or an economic recession affect real estate markets. A rise in interest rates from the historically low levels we experienced at the turn of the millennium will raise the cost of home ownership. But over the long haul, real estate has been a great investment for many people.

However, changes in the national economy can affect a short-term fix-it-and-flip-it strategy. As you search for properties and plan the renovations, don't operate in a vacuum; keep an eye on the national economy. If you purchase property at the start of a downturn in the economy, this makes it harder, but not impossible, to sell the property for a profit during the slump. If this is the case, you can alter your strategy from fix it and flip it to fix it to occupy or fix it to rent.

As you read this chapter, you certainly must be aware of the change in the real estate market since the middle of 2007. Before that time, the market was red hot in most regions of the country. Just about everything you read in newspapers and magazines and saw on TV shows was extolling real estate. Articles and shows told of buyers bidding against one another to pay full price and more. Credit was easy to come by, and a good bit of speculation fueled the market. All this tended to hide the risk involved in real estate investment.

In the previous chapters, we talked about leverage as one of the advantages available to those investing in property. This leverage magnifies the potential profit, but it also exposes you to increased risk. Today the national market has changed from a seller's market, where demand runs ahead of supply, to a buyer's market, where there is more property for sale than there are buyers who want to purchase it.

In a seller's market, the shortage of property compared to ready buyers drives up prices. Buyers will pay top dollar and cannot afford to be picky because there is someone behind them who is willing to purchase the property. For the investor, it's easy to sell the property but difficult not to overpay for new property. Of course, the opposite is true in a buyer's market. Buyers can be picky, as they are not forced to compete with other buyers for the property—there is plenty for sale.

We think that in the next decade, purchasing property to improve will be easier, since the hysteria has been shaken out of the market. If you make the right improvements and control your costs, you'll find many investment opportunities. You are, however, going to have to look longer to find financing and work harder at controlling your costs.

Regional Market

Within the United States at any given time, there are different regions of the country that are experiencing unique real estate markets. Depending on where you are located, your regional market may be different from the markets in other regions of the country. What is happening in California is not necessarily what is happening in the Midwest.

Be aware of your regional real estate market. Property that was purchased at a bargain price in a hot market may not be such a bargain if the regional market cools down. For example, in the mid-1980s, we relocated from the Midwest to the East Coast. The particular area we settled in was experiencing a red-hot market. In fact, our purchase offers were passed over for full-price offers with no mortgage contingency. Less than a year later, the market cooled off, and it was not until the mid-1990s that it gained that much steam again. If you purchased property at the peak of that overheated market, you experienced little or no appreciation during the time the market was flat.

It's difficult, if not impossible, to time the real estate market, which usually doesn't swing as fast as the equity markets, so it's important that you keep regional economic conditions on your radar screen to realize the full potential of your investment. If you are planning on investing in another part of the country, subscribe to a local newspaper or go online on a regular basis to get a feel for the local conditions. Even today, with a national slowdown in real estate, there are still regions of the country that are seeing appreciation.

Local Market

The camera zooming in on the individual houses in a neighborhood is exactly how most people in the real estate market look for a house. The neighborhood in which a potential investment is located is a key factor determining that property's value. There will always be the good and bad sides of the tracks. Entire neighborhoods can change and be revitalized, but this doesn't happen overnight. Purchasing fix-up property in a transitional neighborhood before it is clear that the neighborhood is on an upswing is speculation, and many investors have made tremendous profits doing it. But others, like us, are willing to buy property in a premium neighborhood because we know that when it is improved, it will command a premium price. Good schools, low crime, good transportation, and economic growth greatly influence the value of property.

Comparing Properties

Most professional real estate agents that you establish a relationship with will do what is called a comparative market analysis at no charge. This analysis is an examination of house sale records in recent weeks or months to determine what prices houses of a given size, location, and general condition have been listed at and what their actual selling prices were. When you are looking at these comps, don't forget to factor in the neighborhood.

To understand what buyers expect in a house selling for the price you want to receive for your investment property, look at the characteristics of similar properties that have recently sold. For example, if you buy a house for $150,000 and hope to resell it for $200,000, you will have to change the property to meet the expectations of buyers shopping for $200,000 houses. The difference between the characteristics of $150,000 houses and those of $200,000 houses tells you about the size, features, and condition of the higher-valued property.

Most real estate companies have their own Web sites, with handy search tools that allow you to screen properties on a wide variety of criteria. Filter your search to display property with sales prices close to $200,000. You may have to visit several sites to make a comprehensive list. The difference here is that you will have access only to the asking prices, not to what the properties actually sold for.

Get the Facts

The decision to purchase is made on the individual property, but the decision is not made in a vacuum. Several factors—location, the size of the property, its features and condition, how it compares with similar properties, and how many similar properties are available—must be taken together to determine the value of the property.

Location

The location of a property is one of the most important factors in determining its value. You must compare properties that are in the same location. All other factors being the same, similar properties located in different areas can have vastly different values. Differences in location, even in the same general area, will affect value. For example, a property that is located at the edge of what is considered a good neighborhood may be several thousand dollars less expensive than a property that is located squarely within the neighborhood.

There is also the possibility that the lower-valued location will become highly valued. The more unlikely it is that this will happen, the bigger the difference in price. Investing in up-and-coming locations can be very rewarding, but we have left this to the more aggressive. Just remember that when you compare investments, their locations must be considered comparable.

Size

A major factor in evaluating a property is its size. All other factors being equal, the larger the property, the more valuable it tends to be. The size of the lot and the number of bedrooms and bathrooms must all be considered when comparing several potential properties.

Condition

The condition of the house is the variable that will probably be hardest to compare. Since you are looking at property that needs TLC, it will be in less than perfect condition. This is difficult, if not impossible, to evaluate before you actually visit the property. So for the initial screening, there is not much you can compare until you actually make an inspection. So go back and go over Chapter 8. Make your lists and then compare.

Features

Garages, porches, fireplaces, and other features like these add to the property's value. Carefully list all the features of each property so that you can ferret out the property with the best overall value.

Once you have the data, you can compare the properties that have recently sold or are valued around the target sales price for the property you are analyzing. How are the properties different? How are they the same? What do the higher-valued or higher-priced properties have that the property you may purchase lacks? The answers to these questions will give you direction as to the best improvements to make to meet the buyers' expectations.

Meeting Buyers' Expectations

Whatever repairs, upgrades, or improvements you make to a house, be sure they meet the local building code requirements. Any violations that were not fixed or repairs that were not made that are identified while selling a house can easily give the buyer second thoughts about the property, not to mention a legal reason to back out of the contract. That said, make repairs and improvements that matter based on comparable houses in the neighborhood.

Make Repairs

We look at repairs the way a kid looks at doing homework: you have to do it to get a passing grade. Teachers expect it as a minimum, and they really like it when you do extra-credit work. A home buyer who is paying market value expects that a house will be in good repair and hires a home inspector to look for deficiencies and report them.

If you're considering buying a house and one of the improvements that's needed is a new roof that will cost $10,000 (and possibly much more if the roof underlayment requires replacement), look at your research about comparable houses. If you find that they sell for $115,000, and you will have to pay $75,000 to $80,000 for the property there's no reason to buy the house. You'll spend way too much money on the roof alone. In our experience, as long as the roof looks OK and passes an inspection, buyers are satisfied. Given the choice among two or more comparable houses, most buyers are unwilling to pay the full premium for a house with a new roof. No doubt the new roof will make the house easier to sell, but few buyers will choose to pay the full $10,000 extra. This is also true for the other systems of the house like the furnace, air conditioner and water heater; if they work and look well cared for think twice before replacing them. On the other hand, energy saving appliances are becoming more desirable with the constant rise in the cost of heating oil, natural gas, and electricity.

Don't Mess with the Structure

Another fact that we have discovered is that costs can easily get out of hand when you start to modify the structure or systems of the house. The easiest and most profitable fix-ups are those that don't require major structural changes like moving kitchen and bathroom fixtures or opening up load-bearing walls and adding rooms outside the original footprint of the building. We have had better success building second-floor dormers or decks or moving non-load-bearing walls. We discuss these in Chapter 14, "Space-Expanding Possibilities."

Certainly it's possible to make major structural changes to a property and increase its value beyond the cost of the upgrade, but we'd consider it only if we were going to live in the property over a period of years so that we'd have a bit of inflation working for us.

Kitchens and Bathrooms

Improvements to kitchens and bathrooms will cost and pay back the most. These are the two key rooms that buyers look at very seriously. Even buyers on a shoestring budget want the best possible kitchen and bathrooms they can get. We've never bought a house on which we didn't do a lot of work in both of these rooms because—let's face it—they are the most used rooms in a house. In Chapter 13 you'll find the quick fixes and face-lifts that we think give the best bang for the buck.

The upgrades in a kitchen can range from a basic cosmetic face-lift of paint, flooring, and appliances to expanding the kitchen into an adjoining room and replacing everything from the ceiling to the floor and all the cabinets and appliances.

Even buyers of a two-bedroom home expect at least a full bath and a half bath to handle the crunch when everyone is getting ready for work and school in the morning. So if you use existing space to make a one-bath house into a two-bath house, you'll recoup your investment. In a bathroom, the upgrade can be as basic as scrubbing and wallpapering or gutting the room and rebuilding everything, with a new bathtub and shower, vanity and countertop, tile, and lighting. In some cases, it involves changing the arrangement of fixtures to make a small space work harder.

In Chapter 15 there's information about using the design services offered at home centers to redesign a kitchen or bathroom.

The "Remodeling 2007 Cost vs. Value Report" compares the estimated cost of a professionally installed renovation with the value that it is likely to add to the home a year later. The report indicates that homeowners who invest in a midrange major kitchen remodeling estimated at $55,503 will recover 78 percent, and those who undertake an upscale major kitchen remodeling at $109,394 will recover 74 percent. A bathroom remodeling costing $15,789 recoups 78 percent of that cost. The addition of a bathroom for $37,202 that is built within the existing footprint of the home comes in at 66 percent (source: Remodeling Online).

If you're living in the house while making improvements and the neighborhood will support a luxury bathroom or a gourmet kitchen, you may be able to rationalize the expense. But do the research and find out whether comparable properties feature high-end upgrades and what they're selling for before you jump in.

Think Green

With energy costs rising, every homeowner will face rising utility bills. Energy efficiency has moved from the tree hugger crowd to Main Street, so consider improving the property's energy efficiency as part of your renovation strategy. Many builders are finding that energy-efficient homes are selling. There is a national awakening to the need to become more energy-independent, and this is spilling over into all phases of our society.

Not only are hybrid cars selling well, but most consumers are well aware of the potential savings from purchasing energy-efficient appliances. There are major lending institutions like Citigroup Inc., Bank of America Corp., and JPMorgan Chase & Co. that are offering rebates on closing costs or offering larger loans to those who purchase energy-efficient new homes. Don't overlook programs to certify remodeled property as "Energy Efficient."

Consider purchasing Energy Star (a government program rating energy efficiency) rated appliances that display the Energy Star tag. Be sure to leave the tags and labels on the appliances so that prospective buyers can learn about their efficiency rating. Refrigerators, hot water heaters, clothes washers and dryers, and setback thermostats that conserve energy are good long-term investments.

Avoid the Extreme

Specialized areas like wine cellars, dedicated gyms, tennis courts, and swimming pools seldom give a good return on the investment—that is, unless they are the norm in the neighborhood. Even if they are, the expense is seldom recoverable.

CHAPTER 10

DOING THE MATH

In the preceding chapters, we have gone over the strategy we use to evaluate a property for its potential as a fix-it-and-flip-it candidate. In this chapter, we do the numbers. However you look at the business of real estate investing, unless you are in the rental business, the profit has to come from the difference between the purchase price and the sales price. The difference must be large enough to cover all costs.

This is a simple formula: (sales price) – (purchase price + costs) = profit. If you look carefully at the three variables in this equation, you realize that each is made up of many smaller variables. Some of these you have direct control over, like the purchase price and the fix-up cost; others, like the sales price, you can estimate, but ultimately the market will set this value. Here's a look at the three variables and how they relate to different purchase scenarios.

Purchase Price

The most important variable in the equation is the purchase price. Much of your potential profit in any real estate project is determined the moment you settle on a purchase price. If you overpay for the property, the added value of your improvements can't be fully realized.

The real challenge is that most property that has any potential will eventually find a buyer. If a buyer who plans to live in the property overpays, he or she has time for the property to appreciate. Improvements made during the occupation are not necessarily made to generate a profit, but rather to improve the livability and the homeowner's enjoyment of living there. Eventually the buyer may get money out of the deal.

You, the investor, on the other hand, must purchase the property at a low enough price to enable you to afford the improvements that are needed if the property is to reach its full market value. If you plan to upgrade the property, you still must have a low enough purchase price so that the revenue from the sale covers the planned improvements and still produces a profit. With this in mind, you must establish a purchase price that we call the "target purchase price" for the property to ensure that you don't overpay.

The target purchase price that you can afford to pay for a particular property may be far from what the seller has in mind. Remember that the true value of any property is what a buyer will pay, not what the seller is asking. This is important to remember, since you eventually will swap places and become the seller of this property.

Costs

The next variables in the profit equation are the costs of purchasing and holding the property, the costs of all planned repairs and improvements, sales costs, and, of course, a profit. Some of these costs are easier to calculate than others. Here is a rundown of the major costs involved in fixing up a property for resale.

Closing Costs

At the closing of a real estate deal, certain costs of the transaction are apportioned to the buyer and the seller. The buyer pays for an appraisal, a survey, property transfer taxes, and legal fees. If the real estate taxes have been paid, then a rebate is given to the seller; if not, the seller pays for his or her share of the tax bill. Of course, you also have to settle up with the bank and pay any fees it requires to execute the loan.

These are but a few of the possible closing costs (see Chapter 11, "Buying the Property," for more details), and they can add up to thousands of dollars. Most of the fees and taxes are set fees or a percentage of the sales price. It is possible to make an accurate estimate of what these costs will be. This may seem like a big project at first, but all the deals you will be making will be of the same type, so after the first exercise, estimating the closing costs for your next project will be easier. A real estate or mortgage broker or the bank that is financing the deal can give you a sample closing statement.

Holding Costs

The holding costs include interest on the loan, property taxes, and utilities. The length of time you plan to hold the property affects these costs. Unless the project can be turned around in a month or so and put back on the market, use a year as the standard holding time. Remember that any fix-it project that takes three or four months to complete may require several more months to sell and that the clock runs until the buyer signs on the dotted line.

We found breaking down the holding cost to a monthly figure to be a great motivator to keep the job on schedule. Knowing that it costs $1,800 per month just to own the property is a great motivator to get the job done. Time is money, and if you take this a bit further, you find that in this case, every day you hold the property costs you $60, or for every hour you haven't sold the property, these holding costs reach into your pocket and remove $2.50.

Repairs and Improvements

These can run the gamut from a simple painting and polishing to a second-floor expansion. It is essential that you have a good idea of what these costs will be. The challenge is that you don't have a lot of time to pull these costs together. If the property has potential, other buyers will be looking at it and may be able to act more quickly than you can.

It is difficult to figure repair costs exactly, but we will give you some help in Chapter 12, "Estimating Fix-Up Costs." In that chapter, we give you some ballpark figures for typical repairs and small projects. Use these as a baseline to develop your own set of costs. In addition, we show you how to use both RSMeans and Craftsman Book construction cost books. These are the same cost-estimating sources that many of the contractors you may hire use when bidding on a job. They are helpful in putting together a quick estimate. The books have general square-foot costs for major remodeling and specific costs for typical repair work and provide additional cost figures for both materials and labor data that can be adjusted regionally.

All real estate purchase agreements have an inspection clause that allows for a home inspection, during which you can get more accurate estimates for the costs of improvements. On the inspection day, go through the house with the inspector and ask the inspector what he or she thinks a problem that he or she has found would cost to fix. Some inspectors will give you advice; others will not. If unexpected problems are found, you can work with the seller to resolve the issues, or you can decide to back out of the purchase agreement.

If there are problems, you can suggest that the seller have them fixed, but remember that you are purchasing a property that needs work; if it didn't, you would not be interested in it. Most sellers are reluctant to spend out of pocket but would rather negotiate on price. Make sure you get current and accurate repair cost figures for a particular defect before you accept any verbal agreement like, "OK, we will knock off a couple of thousand from the price and that should cover it." If the estimate is wrong, you will have to make up the difference. If your offer is very low, there may not be room for negotiation; in that case, be sure to add the cost to your improvement budget. (See Chapter 12.)

The repairs and improvements cost represents a major portion of the project's overall expense. If, after you calculate the total cost, you arrive at an unrealistically low purchase price, some adjustments are in order. In some cases the market will not support a selling price high enough to cover the cost of the repairs and improvements and return a decent profit; if that's the case, it's better to find out before you purchase the property.

Contingency

Like any other business, fixing up property for resale has its risks. This is what the contingency fund is all about. While changing a kitchen faucet seems straightforward, it can get grim if you break a rusted pipe in the wall. Something that was budgeted for $100 suddenly costs $400. The contingency is an important part of the budget because it allows you to anticipate the unexpected and provide sufficient funds if they are needed. Because you include the contingency amount as an expense up front to lower the purchase price, not having the expense of a broken pipe ends up on the bottom line. The older and more run-down the property, the higher the contingency fund should be.

Sales Costs

Every real estate transaction has costs to both the seller and the purchaser. We estimate these costs separately because the value of the property when you buy it and when you sell it is different. The largest component of the sales costs is the commission paid to the real estate broker, which a steady customer can negotiate. Both seller and buyer get the same closing statement, so you can estimate the sales costs.

Profit

This line is considered an expense because the difference between the purchase price and the selling price must contain the profit. The figure is the actual amount of cash that you hope to realize after the dust settles, the property is sold, and all loans and bills are paid. Because most of the money to buy and improve the property comes from the lender, even a small amount of cash profit can represent a hefty return on your investment, namely the down payment. As we said before, leverage works in both directions.

Sales Price

It would be nice if you could add up all the costs, decide on a profit, add the resulting figure to the price paid for the property, and place the property back on the market at this price. You can if you buy the property right. That is what the property analysis worksheet will help you calculate.

Any of the real estate Web sites on the Internet is a good place to take an initial look for comparable properties. The search results will give you a ballpark idea of the value of the house, or at least current asking prices.

As we suggested earlier, your real estate broker can also prepare a market analysis of comparable houses that have recently sold. This list will give you the actual sales price of the properties.

Time

One important variable that is not explicitly stated is time. Owning real estate has costs: interest on the loan, taxes, utilities, and similar items. The longer you own the property, the more costs you incur. But over that same period, most real estate appreciates, and this has historically offset the costs. Unless the local real estate market is very hot, historic appreciation rates over a short time won't cover the holding costs. But if you open that horizon to several years or more, the property can appreciate enough to cover these costs. That is one of the most appealing characteristics of a real estate investment.

But like the overall economy, real estate has cycles, and at the end of 2007, we are leaving an up cycle that saw soaring property prices and low financing costs. What the market will be like for the rest of this decade is difficult to predict, but one thing is clear: except in some tight local markets, we are not likely to see the double-digit property appreciation that was common during the first half of this decade. In the short run, you aren't going to be able to count on price appreciation alone to turn a profit.

Analysis of a Fix-It-and-Flip-It Property

When considering a property that has fix-up but not expansion possibilities, we do the research to find out its value after it has been upgraded. Then, working backward from the estimated improved value selling price, we subtract all costs and profit. This number is the most we could pay for the property and expect to cover the cost of the repairs and sell the property for a profit. This is, of course, not set in stone, but unless we modify the plan, it's the most we'd pay.

The purchase analysis worksheet in Figure 10.1 shows an analysis of a single-story, two-bedroom, 1^1/$_2$-bath home in poor condition. Let's say that after completing a market analysis of comparable property, we decided that the house would be worth at least $250,000 with repairs and improvements completed. We'd enter that figure in the "Estimated improved value" row, and then we'd subtract estimated costs (for closing, holding, and repairs, which we would estimate; see Chapter 12) of $26,500. We'd anticipate and subtract a $2,000 contingency and an $8,000 profit as well as estimated sales costs of $15,000. The result would be our target purchase price ($198,500). After putting 10 percent down, the standard mortgage would be $178,650.

Remember that this is a worksheet and that there are variables here that can be fine-tuned. If, after working with the numbers, the target purchase price turned out so low that it would be an insult to the seller, we'd probably either pass on the property or make a lowball offer with the data to back up our reasoning. Because the bank would require an appraisal, we would have the appraiser make two reports: one that states the value of the property as is to support the mortgage, and the other with the value of the property after the fix-up.

Then we'd get a short-term loan, second mortgage, or construction loan—however the bank wanted to structure the deal for the estimated improvement cost. The only money we'd have in the project would be the down payment of $19,850. If everything went as planned, we'd expect to make a good return on our investment. The project would be figured on a one-year holding time; if we finished sooner, the holding costs and interest would be less and we'd get a larger profit.

The lower part of the worksheet is an example of what the sale of the property might look like. In this example, the repairs went over budget by $1,000, and the best offer for the property was $246,000. The cash went to pay off the sales costs, closing costs, and overbudget expenses, a total of $42,260. Remember that the bank loaned the money for the purchase and repairs, so these loans were paid off. The net cash from the sale was $25,090. The down payment of $19,850 and the $1,000 overbudget expenses are returned, leaving a profit of $5,240—a nice 26 percent return on our investment. The more work you do yourself, the more of the construction budget you get to pocket.

Figure 10.1 Sample Property Analysis Worksheet: Fix-It-and-Flip-It Property

Estimated improved value		$250,000.00
Closing costs	$1,500.00	
Holding costs	$10,000.00	
Repairs	$15,000.00	
Total expenses		$26,500.00
Contingency	$2,000.00	
Profit	$8,000.00	
Total contingency/profit		$10,000.00
Estimated sales costs		$15,000.00
Target purchase price		$198,500.00
10 percent down	$19,850.00	
First mortgage	$178,650.00	
Construction loan	$26,500.00	
Sale		
Sales price		$246,000.00
Cost		$198,500.00
Gross profit		$47,500.00
Real estate commission	$14,760.00	
Overbudget expenses	$1,000.00	
Holding/construction	$26,500.00	
Total costs		$42,260.00
Net		$5,240.00
Investment		$19,850.00
Return on investment (before tax)	26%	
Cash Flow		
Sale		$246,000.00
Repay first mortgage	$178,650.00	
Repay construction loan	$26,500.00	
Closing costs	$15,760.00	
Cash out		$25,090.00
Investment		$19,850.00
Profit		$5,240.00
Return on investment (before tax)	26%	

Analysis of an Expand-and-Flip-It Property

The same worksheet can be used to analyze a property that will be expanded, but the initial approach would be a bit different. Instead of making a market analysis for the property as it is, you'd make a market analysis of properties that compare to how it will be after the modifications. For example, this analysis is for a two-bedroom, one-bath house that could be expanded into a four-bedroom, two-bath house (Figure 10.2).

Figure 10.2 Sample Property Analysis Worksheet:
              Fix-It-and-Flip-It Property

Estimated improved value		$380,000.00
Closing costs	$3,100.00	
Holding costs	$18,000.00	
Repairs	$35,000.00	
Total expenses		$56,100.00
Contingency	$5,000.00	
Profit	$12,000.00	
Total contingency/profit		$17,000.00
Estimated sales costs		$20,000.00
Target purchase price		$286,900.00
10 percent down	$28,690.00	
First mortgage	$258,210.00	
Construction loan	$56,100.00	
Sale		
Sales price		$375,000.00
Cost		$286,900.00
Gross profit		$88,100.00
Real estate commission	$22,500.00	
Overbudget expenses	$2,800.00	
Holding/construction	$56,100.00	
Total costs		$81,400.00
Net		$6,700.00
Investment		$28,690.00
Return on investment (before tax)	23%	

Cash Flow

Sale		$375,000.00
Repay first mortgage	$258,210.00	
Repay construction loan	$56,100.00	
Closing costs	$25,300.00	
Cash out		$35,390.00
Investment		$28,690.00
Profit		$6,700.00
Return on investment (before tax)	23%	

We determined that the modified house could be sold for at least $380,000. The worksheet would be used to calculate a target purchase price in exactly the same way as it was with the fix-it-and-flip-it property to calculate a target purchase price. After accounting for all expenses, the worksheet helps us determine that we should not offer more than $286,900 for the property if we expect to meet the profit goal. You can see that the estimated costs for repairs and remodeling are much higher than for a repair-only property. Copy the property analysis worksheet in Figure 10.3 and use it for your own analysis. The math is straightforward here, but an Excel sheet, which will do the calculations for you, is available on the CD-Rom of the companion workbook.

Figure 10.3 Sample Property Analysis Worksheet:
Fix-It-and-Flip-It Property

Estimated improved value	_____
Closing costs	_____
Holding costs	_____
Repairs	_____
Total expenses	_____
Contingency	_____
Profit	_____
Total contingency/profit	_____
Estimated sales costs	_____
Target purchase price	_____
10 percent down	_____
First mortgage	_____
Construction loan	_____

Sale   _____

Sales price   _____

Cost   _____

Gross profit   _____

Real estate commission   _____

Overbudget expenses   _____

Holding/construction   _____

Total costs   _____

Net   _____

Investment   _____

Return on investment (before tax)   _____

Cash Flow   _____

Sale   _____

Repay first mortgage   _____

Repay construction loan   _____

Closing costs   _____

Cash out   _____

Investment   _____

Profit   _____

Return on investment (before tax)   _____

Putting It All Together

Purchasing the property at the right price is the single most important element of being a successful real estate investor because it's difficult to make money on a property you paid too much for. While the hot market in the past may have bailed out investors, it's not wise to count on price appreciation alone to make a profit.

Go back over your property profiles, check the list of required repairs, use the tools in Chapter 12 to get a good handle on the cost of renovations, and then do careful research to determine how much value the improvements will actually add to the property. If you plan on doing some or all of the work yourself, the potential profit may be larger, and if you sell the property yourself, there will be more profit. The key point to remember is: if the numbers don't work out on a property, take a pass. There's always another good house deal down the road.

CHAPTER 11

BUYING THE PROPERTY

After you have ferreted out promising properties, analyzed their potential, and selected the best of the bunch, you still have to purchase the property before you can implement your plan. This process can be as simple as a handshake and an exchange of money for title to the property. More likely, there will be a large cast of professionals who are involved in the purchase in one way or another. If you have already purchased a piece of property, you may have already been exposed to this cadre. Nevertheless, you should be familiar with just what is involved in a typical real estate deal. Here is a rundown on what the players do.

The primary way brokers make their money is by listing property (this is a broker's bread and butter) and receiving a commission or percentage of the sales price when it is sold. Another way they make money is by selling other brokers' listings and receiving a commission. When a broker sells property that he or she listed, that broker takes the lion's share. The office of the listing agent also gets a percentage, which covers the office's costs of doing business, advertising, and so on. So at a property closing, many checks are cut dividing up the agreed-upon selling price of the property. The amount of commission paid to brokers varies depending on the state in which they are licensed; in general, it is 3 to 7 percent of the selling price.

Investing in real estate introduces you to a cast of financial and housing professionals—bankers, loan officers, appraisers, home inspectors, and insurance agents—and all of them will require your attention. They present you with requests for information and forms to fill out, either in person or online. The process is orchestrated by your real estate broker, who keeps things on track and ensures that all the paperwork and processing are completed so that the closing happens on time and with all the parties happy.

So, you've screened several properties, run the numbers on all of them, and found a house that's below the market value and ripe for rehabbing. You have done your homework about getting a mortgage; you have all your financing lined up, and you're ready to make an offer. Here's what to expect.

Doing the Deal

First, you make an offer to purchase the property. Listen to the advice of your broker, but remember your target purchase price; don't be afraid to make a low offer. If the property is new on the market, you may not have much leverage, but if it's been for sale for a month and no one's made an offer, perhaps the market has softened. The seller can either accept your offer or make a counteroffer (asking you to up the ante and pay more), and you can meet the higher price by either accepting it or countering with another offer.

The volleying between offers and counteroffers is where the agent's negotiating skill comes into play and where he or she earns the money you are paying him or her. In addition to the selling price, the terms of the contract can also be negotiated. For example, if you make an $225,000 offer for a property and you want to close the deal and take possession in two months, this might trump an offer for $227,000 if the other buyer's closing date is four months away. Finalizing the sale, getting the money, and moving may be worth more to the seller than selling for a larger amount. You and the seller may agree to a lower price for the property based on the estimated cost of the repairs or replacements specified in the home inspection report, which can be to your advantage.

You may offer cash as an incentive to the seller, so that waiting for financing and approval isn't necessary. A cash offer translates into a fast sale, which can be very enticing to a seller who is leaving the area and wants to move quickly.

Yes, you should have some wiggle room in negotiating the price with the seller, but don't stray from your target purchase price for the property. Know your limit and stick to it, and don't let your emotions get in the way. Just remember that there will always be another house that's ripe for rehabbing.

Leave Yourself an Out

Make sure that any contract you sign has two contingency clauses. One clause should let you out of the deal if the property doesn't pass an inspection and you and the seller can't agree on how to resolve the problem. Unless you make a cash offer, a mortgage contingency is also necessary. This clause states that the purchase is contingent on your obtaining a reasonable mortgage in a stipulated period of time. Many contracts have a provision in which the terms of the mortgage are stated. Make sure that you can live with the interest rate and time frame that are given. A high interest rate or a very long time to secure financing may prevent you from using this clause to back out of the deal. If you can't secure favorable financing, don't purchase the property.

The contract should state that the down payment or earnest money is deposited in an account and that this money is applied to the sales price if the deal goes through but is returned to you if the deal falls apart.

If you haven't already been approved for a mortgage to cover the cost of the property, that's the next step. This is covered in Chapter 6, "Finding the Money." After that, your next step is hiring a home inspector to examine the physical condition of the house and property and make a written report of its condition, including any defects and possible future problems. When the inspection is completed and the inspector reports that the property is sound, you've bought yourself a house.

Hiring a Home Inspector

There are two trade groups representing home inspectors, and a visit to their Web sites to familiarize yourself with the guidelines for a proper inspection and to know what to expect from one is a good idea. At ashi.com, you'll find information about the American Society of Home Inspectors; nahi.org is the site for the National Association of Home Inspectors. Membership in these groups means that the inspector has an expertise in home construction and agrees to a certain standard of conduct. For between $300 and $500, an inspector will make a thorough examination of the property and give you an itemized report of what he or she found.

You can use these Web sites to locate a home inspector in your area, or you can get a reference for an inspector from someone who has bought a home in the area. Many banks, lenders, and real estate brokers suggest inspectors that they work with on a regular basis.

When you call to schedule an inspection, ask if the inspector carries insurance to cover any mistakes that he or she might make and if some or all of the structural and mechanical systems of the house are examined. Schedule the inspection so that you can attend, and ask questions as you go through the house. This is a good time to review your notes about the condition of the house and your planned improvements. If the inspector points out problems, ask for recommendations on how to correct them.

Going to Settlement: Closing the Deal

Do you need a lawyer to represent you when you are buying a house? Maybe yes, maybe no. But if you are purchasing your first home, it's a good idea to hire one to represent your interests and thoroughly explain the process before it happens. If any problems arise, a lawyer can expedite the issue and move the deal to closure. Don't choose just any lawyer; select one that specializes in property closings. You don't need a trial lawyer who is good in the courtroom; you want someone who is well versed in property settlements in the area in which the house is located.

Many law offices hand off this work to a paralegal who goes through the process regularly. Ask friends or your broker for references, and talk to them about what the lawyer charges and what services he or she provides.

Closing Costs for You the Buyer

After you have applied for a mortgage, the lending institution is required to send you a good-faith estimate of your closing costs and confirm the percentage rate of the loan. The closing costs associated with buying a house cover a laundry list of taxes, insurance, reports, searches, and charges for document preparation, tax service, notary service, and state recording fees.

The bank or lending institution holding the mortgage on the property requires most, if not all, of these documents at the closing. These charges and fees add up to about 5 percent of the purchase price of the property.

Current Survey

The survey is a legal description of the property that notes its lot size and boundary lines. A survey team will go to the property and check the boundaries of the lot and the placement of the house and other buildings. If the property has been sold in the past couple of years, you may be able to save some money by purchasing a certified copy of the survey from the survey company.

Appraisal

An appraisal is an estimate of the value of the property by an expert that confirms for the lender that you haven't paid too much for the property by comparing it with other houses in the neighborhood. The insurance company may also want a copy of the appraisal to make sure that the property warrants the level of coverage in the homeowner's policy.

Insurance Binder

The lender also wants confirmation that you will protect the value of the property by taking out an insurance policy. A letter or fax from the insurance broker stating that you have purchased a policy may be all that is necessary. Also, most lending institutions require that they be made a beneficiary of the policy.

Pest Inspection

In most parts of the country, especially in the South, a pest inspection is required. This report states that the property is free of termites or other pests.

Loan Points

The loan points, the fee that lenders charge based on a percentage of the loan, will be stated beforehand by the lender. Points are payable at closing or in some cases can be added to the loan amount. There may also be an escrow fee for holding the escrow account and processing the paperwork for the loan.

Property Taxes

Property taxes are divided up between the buyer and seller based on the time of year of the transaction. For example, if the property is sold on the first of July, then the tax bill is split; each party will own the property for six months. The seller pays half of the taxes, and the buyer pays the other half. At other times of the year, the taxes are divided proportionally. If the seller has already paid the taxes, the buyer' reimburses the seller for the portion of the taxes that the buyer should pay.

In areas where the taxing authority fiscal year does not begin in January the taxes are divided up using its fiscal year. In most areas the taxes are assessed but the tax bills may not be sent out until several months later. In any of these cases the taxes are equitably apportioned according to the time of ownership.

Title Insurance

Title insurance is used to ensure that the buyer is receiving clear title and ownership. The title company also checks to ensure that there are no liens recorded against the property and researches the public records to furnish an abstract confirming that the buyer is receiving free and clear title. In some states, a Torrens certificate is issued instead of a title and provides a registration of title to the property. A prepayment of mortgage insurance, if required by the lender, is included in the closing costs.

The Closing

Between the time when an offer is accepted and the property closing, there are several tasks that have to be performed. A good broker will act as the clearinghouse for these items, but the buyer should be aware of all that's required. Use the checklist in Figure 11.1 to guide you through the process.

Before closing, make arrangements with the utility companies that supply electricity and water to the property to have the accounts transferred to your name. The day before or the day of closing, arrange for a final inspection and walk-through of the house and confirm that all systems are in working order, or at least in the condition that they were in when you saw the property during your last visit.

At a typical property closing, all the parties sit around a large table and sign a pile of papers, most of which were just mentioned. Bring a driver's license to prove who you are, certified checks based on the settlement sheet, and your personal checkbook, just in case there are any last-minute fees required.

A good broker will shepherd you through the process and act as a go-between for you, the loan officer, and the seller's broker. But take the time to review the closing costs and make notes to ask any questions you have. Remember that time is money and you don't want the property settlement delayed, so make sure that all the paperwork is being processed. Check with the loan officer about any outstanding issues that need to be settled, and confirm that the insurance company has submitted a copy of your policy. Find out how your checks should be made out (separate or lump sums), and get certified checks for the exact amounts.

Figure 11.1 Buyer's Checklist

- Order a home inspection of the property.

- Review closing cost estimates.

- Make money transfers to escrow account.

- Order property appraisal.

- Order title search.

- Consult lender about progress of loan.

- Order home insurance.

- Order title insurance.

- Schedule final walk-through.

- Consult with utility companies about changing names on service records.

- Review final settlement statement.

- Get checks issued for settlement.

- Get address of settlement location.

CHAPTER 12

ESTIMATING FIX-UP COSTS

In order to make a rational judgment to invest in a property, you must have a handle on the cost of the improvements you plan to make. In Chapter 10, we run through the decision process and provide a worksheet that shows you how to arrive at the price you can afford to pay for the property while making a profit. In this chapter, we show you how to come up with an accurate estimate of what your planned improvements will cost.

First of all, it's useful to understand how a contractor comes up with an estimate for a specific project. Most contractors who have been in business for any length of time refer to past jobs. If they keep good payroll records, they know the amount of labor required to perform specific jobs, and they know the local cost of skilled labor like carpenters, electricians, and plumbers. They call their local suppliers to get the latest material costs and sit down and compile a bid.

Many pros rely on material and labor cost data compiled by major publishers like RSMeans and Craftsman Book Company to help them put together their bids. These publishers have been collecting construction cost data and compiling them into books and software for years. You can purchase these materials and use them yourself to quickly make accurate estimates of how much your planned renovations will cost.

We'll walk you through an example using the Craftsman Book Company's *2007 National Home Improvement Estimator* (see Figure 12.1).

Figure 12.1

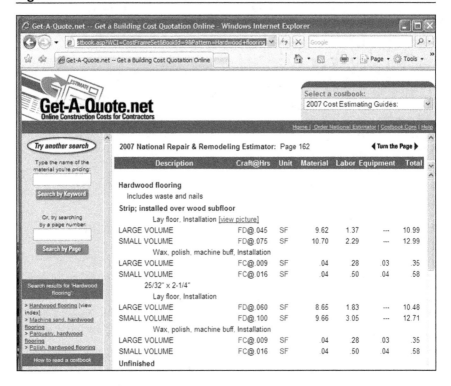

To see samples of the information in the book, visit the company's Web site, www.get-a-quote.net.

You can use Repair & Remodeling Cost Data from RSMeans in the same way. Both have chapters explaining just how to use the data.

The *2007 National Home Improvement Estimator* comes with an estimating program called National Estimator on a CD in the back of the book. Installing this program makes using the data in the book easier, but the book has a very good index for finding information. The program basically uses two windows. One window displays the cost data, and the other gives the estimate. For example, if you type a topic like "tub surround" into the search form, the program shows a listing of all related topics (see Figure 12.2). Click on a topic folder and it opens to show which pages the information is on. Click on the page folder and it displays different styles of tub surrounds and their data in the cost window.

Figure 12.2

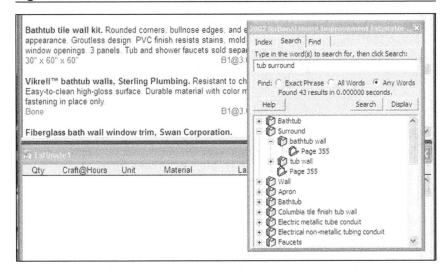

You choose an item in the cost window and use Windows's copy and paste functions to place it in the estimate window. The program asks questions such as how many or how much of the item you need (see Figure 12.3), then instantly copies the information into the estimate window and keeps a running total (see Figure 12.4).

Figure 12.3

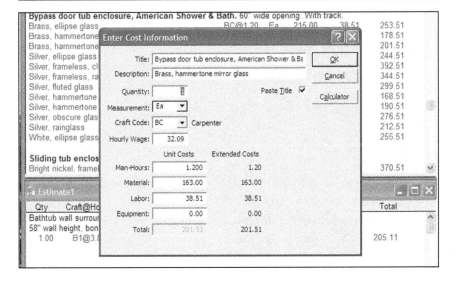

Figure I2.4

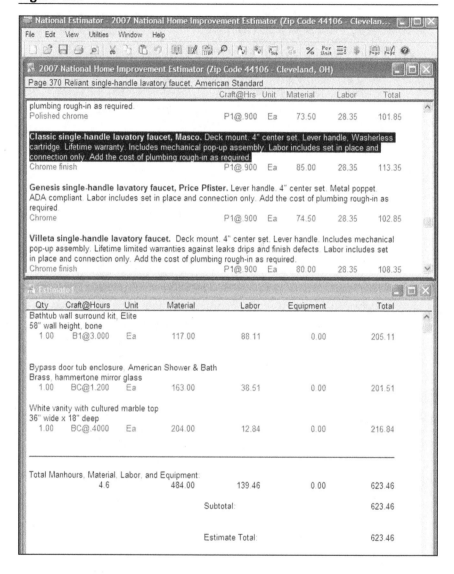

After you have searched out and chosen all the elements that make up the bathroom remodeling, you will have a complete estimate of the labor and material cost for this project (see Figure 12.5). The program will print out the estimate, or you can export it to other spreadsheets or word processing programs.

Figure 12.5

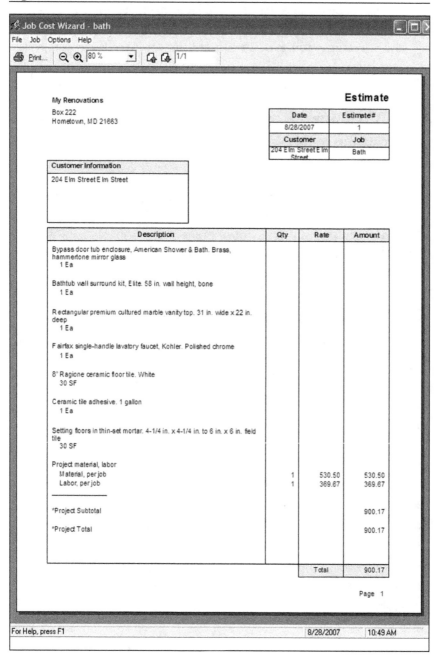

The cost data used by this program are national averages, but the software allows you to tailor the figures to local conditions using a zip code. With a little practice, you will be able to quickly come up with a reasonably accurate estimate of the cost of fixing up the property you plan to purchase.

In addition, you can find hundreds of project costs at the online version of our column, "Do It Yourself . . . Or Not?" at www.diyornot.com. The do-it-yourself (DIY) cost of projects is based on national average costs from major retailers in the Northeast, Southeast, Southwest, Midwest, and West/Mountain regions of the country and e-commerce Web sites with home-improvement products. The Pro cost is determined by averaging the cost and data information from the estimation sources we just described.

To give you more specific cost information, we've included Table 12.1, which lists cost adjustments for many major cities. For example, if you live in or around Chicago, Illinois, the costs given in this chapter should be adjusted by 110.9 percent (regional costs = national cost – 1.109).

Table 12.1 Cost Adjustments for Major Cities

City	Percent	City	Percent
Atlanta	88.4	Memphis	85.7
Baltimore	91.6	Milwaukee	101.2
Boston	116.7	Minneapolis	109
Buffalo	102.3	Nashville	85
Chicago	110.9	New Orleans	85.4
Cincinnati	92.5	New York	133.9
Cleveland	101.9	Philadelphia	111.9
Columbus	94.1	Phoenix	90.2
Dallas	86.7	Pittsburgh	102.5
Denver	93.6	San Antonio	83.7
Detroit	104.3	San Diego	107.1
Houston	89.3	San Francisco	124.2
Indianapolis	95.4	Seattle	104.6
Kansas City	98.6	St. Louis	102.7
Los Angeles	110.6	Washington	96

Source: Do It Yourself . . . Or Not?

When we analyze the work required for an investment property, we look at the cost of the improvement projects and ask ourselves whether we should do the work ourselves or hire out the job. In general, we practically always do the grunt work, which we jokingly refer to as the "mindless tasks" that require little in the way of tools and talents. These are jobs like removing wallpaper, cleaning out a basement, insulating an attic, or pulling weeds—all tasks that anyone with a strong back and a sense of adventure can perform successfully.

Projects

Many of the houses we work on require upgrades to the electrical and plumbing systems. For these jobs, we hire licensed professionals—electricians and plumbers—who will do the job in a workmanlike and timely fashion. When a house requires inspection, we want it to pass with flying colors the first time around, and using seasoned pros has always been a worthwhile investment.

But many jobs are not brain surgery, so a handy investor can do some or all of the work him- or herself. It's sweat equity plain and simple. As you read about the various projects, you'll notice that we let you know when it's absolutely necessary to hire a pro and when you can do some or all of the work yourself.

Because finding some of these specialists isn't always easy, we include how they are listed in the Yellow Pages, a useful resource for contacting them about specific projects.

The cost of materials and labor is one issue; another is the tools and equipment needed for rehabbing a house. At the end of this chapter, you'll find a list of our pet rental tools and why we're fans of our local rental center. But first, let's get started on all the projects you might encounter while rehabbing a house.

Cleaning

Often a house will have a depressed asking price because it's just plain dirty. A little dirt can be overcome, but when it's combined with mildew and lingering pet and/or smoke odors and the house is filled with furniture and debris, a lot more than elbow grease is needed. General housecleaning services range upward of $15 an hour; you'll find them listed in the Yellow Pages under "House Cleaning." Table 12.2 includes the cost of several additional cleaning projects.

These services run the gamut from individuals to commercial franchises. If the house has been neglected and requires more than simple cleaning, there are specialists in fire damage and restoration who can repair damage and administer antimildew and antibacterial treatments to houses.

Table 12.2 Costs of Cleaning Projects

Project	Service	DIY
Power-wash a deck	$125	$75
Wash windows	$245	$16
Clean furnace ducts	$504	$30

Carpet

To clean about 500 square feet of carpeting, a carpet-cleaning service charges about $200. You can rent a rug-cleaning machine for $40 a day, plus $20 more for the cleaning solution. While there's a steep cost difference, consider using a service if the carpeting has stains or pet odors;

LESSONS LEARNED

To protect freshly cleaned carpeting in a house that's on the market, we invest in new paper/plastic-backed drop cloths and cut them in strips about 24 inches wide to serve as runners. We lay them down on a path from the front and back doors and throughout the rooms. This is a subtle suggestion for those viewing the house to follow, and it prevents a trail of dirty, wet footprints on freshly cleaned carpeting. Realtors have told us that this says a lot about our sense of pride in our workmanship.

---

a do-it-yourselfer can tackle routine cleaning, but for stubborn stains and pervasive odors, it's better to hire a professional. We schedule this work at the end of the job sequence, once all the painting has been completed and just prior to putting the house on the market or moving in.

Exterior

Outside power washing can transform dirty siding or a mildew-covered deck or patio in a matter of hours. In the Yellow Pages, the service is listed as "Pressure Washing," but it is divided into businesses that clean buildings ("Building Cleaning-Exterior") and those that specialize in decks and other outdoor structures ("Cleaning Systems-Pressure, Chemical").

A service will charge about $340 to clean the siding exterior of a 1,200-square-foot house, but you can rent a power washer for about $75 a day and do the job yourself if you like working in a wet environment (more about rental tools later in this chapter).

If the house is historic or has loose or damaged siding, think seriously about hiring a specialist to do the job because the powerful blast of the unit can be harmful. If the house has two stories, budget more to rent scaffolding so that you can work on the upper level of the house safely.

A power washer is the tool to use to remove mildew and dirt from a deck. After washing the deck, it's a good idea to protect it with a water sealer or repellent. If both the siding and a deck need cleaning, it's a good bet that you can hire a pro to do the job in one day—something to consider if you're looking for an excuse not to do it yourself.

Chimney

A chimney sweep charges $100 to $150 to inspect and clean a typical two-story fireplace chimney, depending on the degree of creosote buildup and whether there's an insert or an oddly shaped flue to work in. Safety experts say that a chimney should be cleaned every year to eliminate the buildup of creosote, which can lead to a chimney fire. The investment is a good one, especially if a house is old and you cannot judge the condition of the chimney.

Schedule the cleaning early in a rehab project to keep a cloud of chimney dust and soot from damaging freshly painted walls or clean carpeting. Make sure the hearth is protected with two drop cloths, one on the bottom to protect the floor, and the other on top to pick up the soot and debris that falls from the chimney into the hearth.

Roll-Off Containers

When a house is left filled with materials such as old carpeting, appliances, and furnishings, you need to remove them before you can clean anything. Figure about $250 for the cost of having a small roll-off container or Dumpster delivered and then removed when it's filled. Check with your local landfill to see if there's an additional dumping charge. Also check with the local building department to learn if there are time restrictions or other regulations on having a Dumpster sitting in front of a property.

Make sure you're at the property when the Dumpster is delivered so that you can have it' positioned correctly. When these monsters are dropped off their truck, they can damage the pavement or the ground surface. You should be there to be certain that the Dumpster's location isn't infringing on a neighbor's property or damaging the lawn or driveway of your property.

Carpentry

There are many carpentry jobs involved when remodeling or repairing a house, and there are many specialists who perform them. See Table 12.3 for examples of carpentry projects and their costs. A finish or trim carpenter has the skills, tools, and experience to install many different materials and components of a house—woodwork and moldings, paneling, flooring, shelving and built-ins, doors, and windows. In most cases he or she has come up through the ranks of the trade and is skilled in using woodworking tools and techniques. Some trim carpenters specialize in old and traditional houses and are adept at re-creating intricate wood trim, which is sometimes necessary when rehabbing.

Table 12.3 Costs of Carpentry Projects

Project	Carpenter	DIY
Replace a medicine cabinet	$199	$160
Install a 10-foot post-form laminate countertop	$383	$145
Replace a 5-foot-wide sliding mirror closet door	$200	$140
Install a granite 37-inch-wide vanity countertop	$278	$210
Install a towel bar	$80	$45
Replace a 24-inch by 36-inch casement window	$285	$235
Install a 10- by 12-foot suspended ceiling	$225	$115
Install polystyrene molding	$208	$90
Install a fireplace mantel	$1,518	$1,300
Install solid shelving in a closet	$455	$350
Install a stair handrail	$232	$40
Install a tubular skylight	$378	$210
Add a glass block window	$495	$245

You'll find that carpenters charge a range of prices, but few of them work for less than $25 an hour. Many general contractors have carpenters with various levels of skill on their staff.

If the carpentry work required involves several small jobs, consider hiring a handyperson, a jack-of-all-trades, who can evaluate, estimate, and complete small home repairs. You'll usually find them advertised in local newspapers, and they are listed as "Handyman Services" in the Yellow Pages. If there's a bulletin board in a hardware store or home center, you may find their business cards posted.

Plan to call a handyperson service when you have more than one job because often they charge a minimum fee to cover the expense of traveling, and you should make it worthwhile for both you and the handyperson. Make a list of projects so that the handyperson can make all the installations and small repairs in one trip. This works out to both your advantages.

Another option for hiring a carpenter is to use the installation service for building materials, appliances, and fixtures offered at many lumberyards and home centers. This turnkey service, created for consumers who don't have the time or can't find references for tradespeople, also works nicely for a real estate investor.

Electrical Work

Some electrical work can be completed by homeowners, but most requires a licensed electrician who is responsible for the workmanship and quality of his or her workers. (See Table 12.4 for examples of electrical projects and their costs.) These are high-priced professionals who get between $50 and $80 an hour. Electricians fall into two categories: they are at either the master or the journeyman level. A master is the higher level; someone at this level is trained and qualified to plan, design, install, and maintain electrical systems. A master electrician knows the National Electrical Code and any state requirements, has passed a test, and has at least two years' experience. A journeyman electrician is licensed by the state to install wiring and equipment. Some states require that a journeyman work with a master electrician.

Table 12.4 Cost of Electrical Projects

Project	Electrician	DIY
Replace a recessed light	$70	$25
Replace a 32-inch ceiling fan	$207	$160
Replace an 8-foot, 4-head low-voltage halogen track lighting system	$183	$140
Replace a porch light	$83	$40
Install a bathroom light/vent	$256	$140
Replace a light fixture	$101	$45
Replace a doorbell	$144	$38

Note that these projects are replacements, so a homeowner who has experience working with electrical projects can safely complete them.

LESSONS LEARNED

Don't be tempted to hire a freelance electrician or one who works on the weekend at a lower rate. When it comes time for the property to be inspected, if the work is unsatisfactory, you won't have much recourse except to hire a licensed pro to redo the work—certainly not a way to cut costs.

You'll find electricians in the Yellow Pages under the "Electrical Contractors" listing. If you have the opportunity to evaluate an electrician's work before hiring him or her, here are a few things to look for. Electric outlets and switch plates should lie flat on the surface of walls and be plumb and square, not tilted. At the service panel, wires and cables should run straight, not be tangled or crossed. In a basement or attic, check to see that wires are attached firmly to the framing at regular intervals.

As we mentioned earlier, you can use a retailer's installation service when buying electrical fixtures or appliances. The retailer arranges for an electrician to do the installation and is responsible for both the scheduling of the job and, of course, your satisfaction.

Flooring

Although we've always thought that a fresh coat of paint can do more than anything else to transform the appearance of the rooms in a house, new or refinished flooring is a close second. Together, they provide a dramatic makeover. Our best experience has been buying all the flooring material for a house from one flooring dealer. We make one trip to the flooring store with all the room measurements and see what's available. The installer likes to make one trip to the house and do all the flooring at the same time. We let the retailer determine how much material is needed and then see what the store has on hand. The retailer makes a house call to confirm our dimensions and check out the condition of the floor and subfloor.

Boring can be beautiful. Don't be tempted by a low price on a good-quality fuchsia carpeting or a wild pattern of resilient material or tiles.

No matter how good the flooring is or what a great price you can get, wild and crazy colors and patterns in flooring material are a turnoff to buyers. Other investors like to shop around and find flooring materials at closeouts. We prefer to find a dealer who has materials we like and good installers, and then stick with that dealer. See Table 12.5 for examples of flooring projects and their costs.

Table 12.5 Cost of Flooring Projects

Project	Flooring Contractor	DIY
Sand, stain, and seal a 14- by 20-foot room	$780	$230
Install a 10- by 15-foot resilient floor	$418	$300
Install a 14- by 20-foot laminate floor	$1,915	$1,100
Tile a 40-square-foot entrance hall	$314	$155
Install 170 square feet of finished parquet tiles	$1,038	$510
Lay carpeting in a 12- by 14-foot room	$792	$360
Install 120 square feet of oak strip flooring	$726	$375
Lay 180 square feet of 12-inch vinyl tiles	$499	$270
Restore a wood floor	$138	$75

Note: These cost estimates are for moderately priced materials. They don't include any repair work or underlayment.

Refinishing Floors

When we work on investment property, the flooring choice comes down to keeping the existing flooring and improving it, or replacing it altogether. If the property has hardwood floors, we refinish them instead of replacing them. The houses we've remodeled have often had oak floors throughout, and they finish up beautifully in a dark or light stain.

The same is true in older historic homes, where the flooring is usually soft pine that cleans up to a rich, golden finish. Unfortunately, old floors have sometimes been painted, and that can be a real challenge, but it's worth the effort.

Speaking of effort, refinishing floors is a job that we hire a professional to do. We've tried doing the sanding and refinishing ourselves with only marginal results, and we've found that hiring a floor sander is a much better idea.

Yes, you can rent a floor sander and do it yourself, but you can also do a lot of damage. The machine is a brute to handle, and there's no place to practice using it. All it takes is one mistake with the machine that gouges the floor and you'll spend any money you may have saved on getting a floor specialist to repair it. If you want to do some of the work, do the finishing after the floor has been sanded, but we've found that handing the work over to a pro gives us the best results.

Carpeting

When a house doesn't have hardwood floors, we opt for wall-to-wall carpeting to make the rooms look spacious and unified, not to mention attractive and easy to clean. We choose a good-quality, tightly woven nylon carpeting in a neutral color and use it everywhere except high-traffic rooms like a foyer, kitchen, bathroom, and utility area. Wall-to-wall carpeting blankets the rooms, reducing noise and providing comfort and insulation.

LESSONS LEARNED

If you want to do some of the grunt work, remove the old carpeting. This low-skill, labor-intensive job is nasty, but it will save you the labor cost of hiring someone.

Resilient Flooring

For high-use rooms like the kitchen, bathroom, and utility room, we install vinyl resilient flooring that blends with the color of the carpeting so that when the two surfaces meet, there's a visual transition separated only by a threshold that conceals the joint at the doorways. Resilient sheet flooring, sold by the yard in 6- and 12-foot-wide rolls, is a good choice for high-traffic areas because it's a tough and durable material. The installation involves several phases: removing the base shoe molding, inspecting the subfloor, cleaning the subfloor (especially at wall joints where dirt and dust accumulate), planning the layout of the material, cutting it to fit, and then installing it. The job is completed with new or reused base shoe molding.

LESSONS LEARNED

Thicker carpet may prevent doors from swinging properly. If this happens, it requires removing the door from its hinges, measuring how much to trim from the bottom of the door so that it will clear the carpeting, and then cutting that amount off the bottom of the door with a saw.

Plastic Laminates

The new laminate or preengineered floors are a popular choice for kitchens and family rooms because they're so good-looking and easy to clean. For an investment property, they are also easy to install. These laminates come in planks, squares, and blocks in faux wood, marble, stone, and granite patterns. The tongue-and-groove materials either are secured together with glue or snap together. At about $5 a square foot, the glueless laminates are pricey, double what the glue-down laminates cost. If the material provides the look and feel you want and you plan to live in the house for a while before selling or renting it, you won't go wrong.

Ceramic Floor Tile

Ceramic tile is a nice material to use in a foyer or entrance hall. A ceramic floor entry provides a durable surface for dirty shoes and snowy boots, yet it can be cleaned easily. When a property is on the market, lay a throw rug on the tiles so that the floor can withstand traffic, not only of prospective buyers but of the team of inspectors and appraisers who eventually have to tour the house. This material's hard surface is also a good choice in a bathroom.

When considering a tile floor, choose a neutral color and pattern that blends well with the adjoining floor surfaces, and make sure that you are looking at floor tile, not wall tile, which is thinner and not slip-resistant. A tile floor is installed with thinset adhesive over a sound subfloor that is level and solid. The joints are sealed with grout to complete the installation.

Most foyers and bathrooms are small spaces, so choose tiles that are scaled to the space. If you're shopping at a flooring center or retailer, you'll find a good selection of floor tiles that you can put together with the carpeting or other materials that you'll be using in the house.

If you are prospecting for a tile installer and inspecting his or her work, take an overview of the tiles to see if the surface is level and the tiles appear balanced and symmetrical. The band of tiles outlining the floor should be about the same size around the room. The grout lines should be straight and even and have consistent spacing, and the grout should be in the grooves, not on the tiles.

Parquet Tiles

On occasion, we've used 12-inch-square prefinished parquet tiles in an entrance; they provide a complementary contrast to adjoining rooms with carpeting. The tiles can be installed over an old wood floor that's been sanded smooth, with any old paint, lacquer, wax, or shellac removed. Old resilient or sheet flooring must be removed and the floor covered with underlayment before parquet tiles are laid.

Underlayment

The key to a good flooring installation is the underlayment or subfloor underneath the material that provides a smooth, level, uniform surface. The material comes in four- by eight-foot sheets in thicknesses from $1/8$ inch to $3/4$ inch, the thicker being the most common. Hardboard underlayment is used over wood or plywood subfloors to bridge gaps and cracks in the floor. Another type of underlayment is frequently used under carpeting, tile, and vinyl flooring. Particleboard, the least expensive of these materials, is an engineered material made of wood particles bound together with resin.

Sometimes we've had to replace the subfloor in a bathroom because we discovered that it had been damaged from a water leak in the toilet—something that became obvious only when the toilet or floor was removed. Water had seeped beneath the floor over time, and the particleboard beneath it had deteriorated.

LESSONS LEARNED

Different floor levels can be an issue and a safety hazard that causes tripping when people walk from one height floor to another. If your plans call for installing a new floor on top of an existing one, make sure that you take the floor thickness into account. You may need to remove a layer of flooring material to bring the new floor down to the same height as the floor in an adjoining room.

Landscaping

In our experience, most of the landscaping work required on investment property involves either planting a few shrubs or removing years of overgrown weeds and plantings. In either case, we think of the landscaping, especially at the front of the house, as a way to enhance curb appeal. See Table 12.6 for examples of landscaping projects and their costs.

Our approach is to spend the minimum required and to work with what's there. We replace bushes when necessary, trim the branches of a sprawling tree, and remove what's overgrown. When it comes to plants, the standard investment we make is a large clay container filled with colorful flowers along with a new welcome mat.

Table 12.6 Cost of Landscaping Projects

Project	Landscaper	DIY
Remove a 2-foot-wide tree stump	$164	$100
Edge a 32-foot garden bed with aluminum edging	$188	$70
Revive a 100-square-foot patch of lawn	$96	$50
Seed a 3,000-square-foot lawn	$230	$190
Plant a 10-foot honeysuckle hedge	$193	$82
Lay a sod lawn	$1,019	$650
Lay a stone garden path	$789	$210
Prune trees and shrubs	$80	$35
Build a rail fence	$1,090	$500
Build a deck	$3,022	$1,600
Build a picket fence	$841	$525
Lay a brick patio	$2,520	$1,100

Often a neglected property is one that's ripe for rehabbing, so we've had our share of "jungle houses," the term of endearment that we use for those that are totally overgrown with weeds and vegetation. Usually we can tackle the work, but if the yard is large and time is of the essence, we'll hire a landscaper who can come in with a crew and get things cut back and under control.

With an overgrown landscape, concentrate on trimming and nurturing what's there and removing what shouldn't be. If you want to participate in the work, landscaping offers an opportunity because it's a good example of grunt work. Garden tools are inexpensive, and you probably already own some. For more heavy-duty projects like removing an eyesore of a tree stump, you'll need to rent a power grinder and a vehicle to transport it.

When a lawn is overgrown and patched with weeds, a few hours with a good lawn mower and trimmer can work wonders. Clumps of weeds, bare spots, and areas of compacted soil are repairable conditions that take time and patience and a few basic lawn tools—more opportunities for a do-it-yourselfer. Any work done to renew a lawn and garden should be followed by a routine of watering.

In general, a landscaping service or individual landscaper charges about $15 to $20 an hour, depending on the scope of the work. You'll find the business cards of independent workers who do yard work posted on the bulletin boards at local lawn and garden centers and see their advertisements in the classified ads or the home section of local newspapers. A landscaping service is a company that does a variety of gardening installations and maintenance work; they are listed in the Yellow Pages under "Landscape Contractors."

The landscaping season depends on the climate in which you're investing, and the weather conditions can either help or hinder your work. Monsoon rains will keep you from landscaping work, as will a drought that produces soil that's hard as clay. So you can plan the work in the yard, but in some cases Mother Nature will control when you do it.

Painting

Painting, the number one do-it-yourself project, will make the most dramatic improvement to a house, investment or otherwise. We like to paint the interior of a house, so we always do it ourselves. (See Table 12.7 for examples of painting projects and their costs.) We usually hire a painting contractor to paint the exterior siding and trim because it requires scaffolding and a lot of ladder work. Inside, we paint all rooms (walls and ceilings) in an off-white latex flat paint and use alkyd-based satin enamel on the woodwork and trim and in the bathroom. We buy the paint in five-gallon pails and use rollers and brushes.

We use a gray or beige latex paint in basements, sometimes using a roller and other times renting an airless spray gun, which we have found does an amazing job of transforming a dirty and dingy space into a clean and usable one. If needed, we use a floor and porch enamel on the floor with a roller on a pole.

Table 12.7 Cost of Painting Projects

Project	Painting Contractor	DIY
Paint the walls and ceiling of a 12- by 20-foot room	$238	$90
Paint 10-foot wood kitchen cabinets	$214	$75
Paint 20- by 20-foot masonry basement walls with a roller	$221	$95
Paint the siding of a 2,500-square-foot house	$714	$155
Paint a 400-square-foot porch floor	$158	$46
Remove varnish from 2 double-hung doors	$289	$40
Remove 2 layers of paint from 1 double-hung window	$318	$45
Paint 500 square feet of paneling	$231	$75
Paint a 100-foot metal rail fence	$124	$35
Stain a 100-foot wood fence	$132	$30

Painting Cover-Ups

If kitchen or bathroom cabinets need a face-lift, we paint them with an oil-based enamel after thoroughly sanding and preparing the surface. We use the same process to conceal ugly wall tile—plastic or ceramic—as long as the tile is sound and not in direct contact with water, like inside a shower or bathtub. And when we find a room with walls covered with dark paneling, we refinish or paint them. There's a real savings when you paint cabinets, wall tiles, or paneling compared with the alternative of removing or replacing them. The key to the cover-up is preparing the surface and priming it so that the paint has a smooth surface to adhere to. For example, wash the surface with a 50-50 solution of household ammonia and water to remove soap film from bathroom walls or grease from kitchen walls. Then use a power sander with 120-grit sandpaper, wood filler, and an alkyd (oil-based) primer. Fill in any nail holes or blemishes in cabinets or paneling with wood filler, and when it's dry, sand the surface smooth. For knots in the paneling, use a spray stain blocker like B-I-N so there won't be any bleed-through of the stain. This is another good example of grunt work that yields a high return on your investment.

Plumbing Work

A licensed plumber should do most of the plumbing work in an investment property because many local building codes require it, and in the end everything must pass inspection. Plumbers charge between $60 and $80 an hour for small projects. They usually work for less on major projects.

That having been said, there are several repairs or upgrades that a handy investor can make if he or she has some plumbing experience and the time it takes to complete them. Plumbing isn't brain surgery, but it's not that simple either. Replacements of most plumbing fixtures, such as a faucet or a garbage disposal, don't require a building permit and are so straightforward that a handy investor can do them. See Table 12.8 for examples of plumbing projects and their costs.

Table 12.8 Cost of Plumbing Projects

Project	Plumber	DIY
Replace a showerhead with a slide bar	$172	$85
Replace a 40-gallon electric water heater	$508	$275
Replace a dishwasher	$574	$550
Replace a washerless bathroom faucet	$165	$100
Install a porcelain pedestal sink and faucet	$700	$450
Replace a single-bowl, 25-inch-wide stainless sink and faucet	$452	$255
Replace a garbage disposal	$241	$120
Replace a toilet	$306	$160
Replace a single-lever washerless cartridge-type kitchen faucet	$160	$125
Replace a pedestal 1/2-hp. sump pump	$223	$120
Replace a laundry tub	$215	$80

You'll find plumbers listed in the Yellow Pages as "Plumbing Contractors," and from their ads you'll be able to see what the scope of their work is. Just as with electricians, you can get an "installed price" at a retailer and have the retailer install the plumbing fixtures.

Wallboard

Wallboard, the material that makes up the walls of houses built after the 1950s, is a commodity item sold in 4- by 8- or 4- by 12-foot sheets or panels. It is heavy to lift and time-consuming to install. See Table 12.9 for examples of wallboard projects and their costs. Wallboard panels have a paper facing over a gypsum plaster core. The panels are screwed or nailed to wall studs, and the joints between them are covered with fiberglass or paper tape and then embedded in compound. The compound is sanded smooth, and another application is made to fill in the voids and create a smooth, seamless surface. This is sanded again and then primed and painted. When painted, the paper facing of the wallboard absorbs some of the paint and dries to a smooth surface.

Table 12.9 Cost of Wall Projects

Project	Professional	DIY
Hang wallboard in a 15- by 20-foot room	$1,095	$280
Repair damaged wallboard	$55	$17
Hang wallpaper in a 14- by 18-foot room	$364	$180
Hang a double border (at ceiling and chair rail) in a 12- by 14-foot room	$145	$75
Remove two layers of painted wallpaper in a 14- by 18-foot room	$392	$50
Tile three walls of a bathtub surround	$563	$165
Tile 8 square feet of a kitchen backsplash	$268	$175
Install wall paneling	$967	$420
Install wood wainscoting	$401	$150
Install a fiberglass bathtub surround	$644	$350

In an investment property, wallboard is most often used to create a room where there wasn't one, such as an attic expansion, or as a replacement to repair damaged wallboard. The most common types used in houses are $^1/_2$- and $^5/_8$-inch-thick wallboard.

There are also specialty types of wallboard. Foil-backed wallboard is used on exterior walls and in high-moisture areas like bathrooms to provide a vapor barrier. Green board also is used in high-moisture areas, and it's the preferred backing for ceramic tile that's not in a tub or shower stall. Cement board—a $^1/_2$-inch-thick board with a cement base, instead of plaster—is waterproof and was created as a base for tile in wet areas.

Wallpaper

Selecting colors and patterns of wallpaper is a very personal choice, so spending a lot of money on it isn't the best investment you can make. See Table 12.9 for examples of wallpaper projects and their costs. If you wallpaper any room, make it the kitchen or bathroom, and choose very neutral colors and patterns. For the best results, use a vinyl-coated, fabric-backed, and prepasted wall covering that is durable, pliable, and easy to hang. To estimate the cost of doing a room, figure that a double roll will cover approximately 56 square feet and cost about $45. You'll find both cheaper and much more expensive options, but that's a ballpark figure to work with.

A less expensive way to add a spark of color to a room is with a wallpaper border, which does a nice job of defining the space in a kitchen or bathroom without overpowering it.

Removing Wallpaper 101

We save a lot of money by removing wallpaper ourselves, a tedious job that's the ideal kind of grunt work for the not-so-handy investor. Tape plastic drop cloths to the baseboard molding around the room to protect the floor. This does double duty when the job's over. The messy, wet scraps of wallpaper are on the drop cloth, so you untape it, wrap it up, and throw it away.

You need a razor scraper, a Paper Tiger (a scoring tool), and a quart of wallpaper remover. You'll also need a bucket and a paint roller to wet down the walls. Score the walls with the Paper Tiger, which penetrates the wallpaper without damaging the surface of the wall behind it. Then apply the remover with the roller so that it gets behind the paper to loosen the adhesive holding the paper to the wall. Use the razor scraper to scrape the paper off the wall.

Instead of chemical wallpaper remover, you can use a wallpaper steamer. You will still need to use the Paper Tiger to create tiny holes in the wallpaper so that the steam can penetrate the paper. Fill the steamer's tank with water and plug it in; when the water begins to boil, steam comes out of the hot plate. As you hold the hot plate to the wall with one hand, you use a wide putty knife or razor scraper in the other to remove the wallpaper.

Wall Tiling

Ceramic tile is a tough, hard-working material that is ideal for covering walls, and we've used it primarily on the three walls surrounding a bathtub. It comes in virtually any color and countless styles, but we usually choose the most basic neutral shades. You can find tile contractors in the Yellow Pages under the listing "Tile-Ceramic-Contractors and Dealers." You can also get an installed price for tile work from many tile retailers and home centers where tile is sold. See Table 12.9 for examples of wall tile projects and their costs.

If you have more than one tiling project for a property, definitely schedule the work for all the projects at the same time so that the tiling contractor can minimize his or her return visits. Tiling work involves several phases. First, the walls are prepared and patched (if necessary), and then the layout of the tiles is planned. Next, the mastic is applied and the tiles are laid. When the tiles have set, then all the spaces between the tiles are filled with grout. When set, the tiles are washed off and the grout is scored.

Tools and Equipment: to Rent or to Own

If you're a real estate investor working on houses to improve them for resale or rental, you can rationalize buying designer power tools. No one (not even the IRS) will question your logic. There are some specialty tools that we use infrequently, so we rent them; others that we use regularly, we buy.

Cordless Drill (Own)

If you don't already own a ⅝-inch cordless drill, buy one; you'll use it repeatedly in making repairs and installations.

Airless Paint Sprayer (Rent)

When we have a large basement with rough walls to paint, we rent an airless sprayer that pumps paint through a small hole in the tip of a spray gun at very high pressure. We've found that spraying walls, despite the intensive preparation time to mask surfaces that you don't want to paint, is a good bet.

Long Ladders and Scaffolding (Rent)

We don't have a good place to store long ladders and scaffolding, so we rent them when they're needed, which is usually for painting. We like A-frame ladders, which are self-supporting and adjustable for painting stairwells and working on ceilings.

Heat Gun (Own)

For less than $75 you can buy your own heat gun, and you'll find it useful on any number of occasions. It's good for removing paint and var-

nish, most definitely, but it comes in handy when you're unfreezing frozen water pipes in the winter and removing adhesive from a floor after
the tiles have been popped off.

Tile Saw (Own)

You can rent or borrow a tile saw wherever you buy tile, but we bought
one so that we would always have it available, and it's proved to be a good
$100 investment. We do small tiling projects like around bathtubs and
sometimes a backsplash, and we like the convenience of always having a
saw available that makes clean, accurate cuts. Because it's not rented out,
we don't have to worry about misaligned cutters or dull blades.

Wallpaper Steamer (Own)

We've taken off more rolls and layers of wallpaper than we care to
remember, and we prefer to own rather than rent a steamer. Granted,
the rental units are for commercial use, so they're bigger and beefier,
but the consumer-grade unit that costs about $50 works just fine to
loosen the paper's adhesive so that it can be scraped off the wall.

Electric Power Washer (Own)

You can buy an electric pressure washer with a pressure range of 1,500
to 2,000 PSI (pounds per square inch) for about $175, and you'll use it
for a variety of cleanup chores. It's ideal for cleaning large, dirty surfaces like a wooden deck or siding. You can easily rent a unit at a rental
center, but having one available when you need it makes it worth the
investment.

Wet/Dry Shop Vacuum (Own)

Investment property is often neglected property, and you'll find that a
shop vacuum makes cleanup chores easier. You'll use it to remove debris
from a dirty garage or basement, and if you're under construction, it'll
make short work of sucking up drywall dust and wood shavings.

Lawn Mower (Own)

Nothing does more to improve the curb appeal of a house than trimming its lawn, so a mower is a must-have tool. Choose one that's easy to operate and transport, and keep its blade sharpened and the engine tuned up.

Please note that the project costs in this chapter are as current as we can make them but in time they will be out of date so use this chapter as a guide. The cost estimating sources we mentioned at the beginning of this chapter are kept current by the publisher and are worth the investment. Since time is money and calculation of the quantity of paint, wallpaper and many of the other materials you will be purchasing is time consuming we have also included easy to use calculator spreadsheets in the workbook to make your estimations accurate, quick and easy.

CHAPTER 13

QUICK FIXES, CLEANUPS, AND REPAIRS THAT MAKE YOU MONEY

To prepare a house for going on the market, stagers are sometimes hired to make the house look and feel better. They remove about one-third of the owner's stuff, mostly personal belongings and clutter, to make the rooms look more spacious. Sometimes Realtors hire a stager to decorate an empty house to give prospective buyers an idea of how it will look furnished.

We have found that buyers are not likely to be impressed by what they can't see. What a prospective buyer does notice is faulty or incomplete workmanship and things that don't work, so spend your time making basic repairs and replacing inexpensive things that show. These improvements tell a buyer that care was given to making the house ready to occupy in move-in condition—just the impression you want to make. Here's our rundown of fast fixes, cleanup chores, and repairs that are easy to do and don't cost a bundle. They add value to the house and make it more salable or rentable.

Decorating

There are quick fixes and decorating ideas that go a long way toward making a house clean, fresh, and inviting. The small investment required for these finishing details makes a house livable and appealing.

Paint

If you do nothing else, paint the rooms. You'll get the most bang for your buck with a $25 gallon of paint because nothing else can make such a dramatic improvement. We use off-white flat latex paint on walls and an eggshell or satin finish on woodwork and trim. By choosing a neutral shade of paint, you give prospective buyers a blank canvas to decorate around. To keep things simple, we paint ceilings and walls the same color. Another benefit of painting is the inviting aroma of a freshly painted house.

TIP: Invest a few bucks in a paint roller handle extension pole so that you can paint the ceilings easily and reach into corners. For a small painting project, we like to paint out of a gallon can using a plastic grid that fits inside it with a mini-roller.

Get a paint spinner, a device that works like an old-fashioned spinning top toy and spins excess paint out of a roller or brush to clean it.

TIP: If you plan to paint the woodwork in a room to match a new wallpaper, paint the trim first, then hang the wallpaper.

Window Blinds

For a finished appearance and to eliminate the fishbowl aspect of an empty house, install miniblinds on the windows. For as little as $10 a window, you can buy one-inch vinyl miniblinds; the aluminum ones start at around $14 each. An inexpensive vertical blind for a patio door costs about $50. Installing these window treatments is easy, especially because you learn by doing and repeating the process.

TIP: If you want to dress up the blinds, add a cornice window topper (painted wood or plastic with padded fabric, sold in kits) to complete the window treatment.

Decorative Window Film

If a window is open to the street and a sense of privacy is needed without blocking the daylight, apply a decorative window film that looks like etched glass. It's as simple as cleaning the glass, measuring and cutting the film, then positioning the film on the glass and using a squeegee to smooth it in place. You'll find the film sold at home and decorating centers in several designs and patterns.

Floor Registers and Heat Grates

Replace any old units that have rusted or that have bent louvers that no longer operate. New registers and grates cost $5 to $10 and are available in a wide range of sizes and shapes. They go a long way toward improving the look and appeal of a room.

Dark Knotty Pine Paneling

Remove the dark finish on old paneling with a gel-type paint and varnish remover. Apply it with a paintbrush and scrape off the finish with a wide putty knife when the remover bubbles and softens. Then clean the paneling with a rubdown of mineral spirits and let it dry. Use an electric finish sander, then vacuum away the dust and apply a water-base polyurethane with a brush or tung oil with a rag.

Electrical Projects

Here are some inexpensive electrical repairs and replacements that give an old house an updated look. These are basic and easy projects that require a minimum of tools and talents. Learn how to do them yourself so that you'll be confident and able to do them later on other investment properties.

Electric Switches and Receptacles

To create a sense of newness and uniformity throughout all the rooms in a house, replace the electric light switches, receptacles, and plate covers. At about $1 each, this is a small investment in an improvement that updates the house. It's a particularly noticeable upgrade if the existing ones have layers of paint or if they are the push-button type found in many older homes.

TIP: Label and number the circuits in the electric service panel box, such as "master bedroom #1,"and mark the corresponding numbers on the inside of the switchplate and receptacle covers in the room.

To comply with the National Electrical Code, replace each electric outlet in the kitchen and bathroom with a GFCI (ground fault circuit interrupter). This device reduces the danger of a deadly shock from a faulty plug-in cord or appliance. It measures outgoing and returning current and shuts off the power if it detects a possible dangerous current imbalance. It has a test button that, when it is pushed in, switches off the power to the outlet and any receptacles connected to it. In addition to the kitchen and bathroom, GFCIs are required in all the wet areas of a house, such as the laundry room, unfinished basement, garage, outdoor areas, or wherever there's construction activity. It's not difficult to replace a standard receptacle with a GFCI (under $15), or you can hire an electrical contractor to do it.

TIP: If you're working in a house and you don't know which circuits power a room, use a portable radio. Plug the radio into an outlet in the room, then turn off all the circuits and turn them on again one by one. When you hear the radio turn on, you know you've found the circuit. This is particularly handy when you're working alone in a two-story house, where it can be a distance from the room to the circuit panel box.

Dimmer Switches

Another easy electrical upgrade is to replace a standard light switch in the dining room with a dimmer switch. This is a nice touch that costs about $15 and creates a cozy feeling in the room. The job involves turning off the power at the main circuit panel, removing the old device by disconnecting and cutting the wires, installing the new switch, reattaching the wires to the terminals, testing the device, and finally turning the power back on.

Test the Switches and Receptacles

If the existing switches and receptacles are OK, check to make sure that they work. Turn on the switches and plug a small lamp or radio into the receptacles. Make a note of any switches or receptacles that don't work and replace them.

Light Fixtures

In many homes there's a hodgepodge of ceiling light fixtures that, although they may work, are distractions instead of attractions. Assess the style and condition of all light fixtures in the ceilings, and replace those that are dated and worn. Don't go overboard with expensive new ones. For the bedrooms, choose a basic $15 ceiling fixture with two bulbs that hugs the ceiling. For a dining room or kitchen, choose a traditional style; there's an amazing selection of fixtures in the $50 range at home centers. The same is true for hall lights. Coordinate the hall, dining room, and kitchen fixtures so that they are similar in style and finish.

Thermostat

Replace an old thermostat with a new one, especially if it has years of paint around its edges. You'll find a standard round device for about $40 and a programmable unit for about $100; either one is a noticeable upgrade.

Internet Connection

We live in a connected world. Just about everyone is online, so consider upgrading the "high-tech" appeal of your property by installing a wireless router that costs less than $50. All you have to do is provide a power source for the router and then run a phone line and cable coax to the router. A new owner can connect whatever high-speed service he or she chooses to the router, and the whole house is then Internet-ready. You may even decide to install a service and have it up and running so that you can offer it as an incentive to purchase.

Walls, Doors, and Windows

We all know that when you enter a room, your eyes immediately go to the hole in the wall or the broken windowpane. Any eyesore usually draws attention, and that's not the impression you want to make on prospective buyers. These repairs cost next to nothing and can be completed in little time. They're all worth doing.

Wall Repairs

The holes in walls left by pictures and decorations look like nasty pockmarks when the house is emptied out. Before painting the walls, spend the time to repair the holes so that the finished surface will be flat and smooth. Look for holes in the walls behind doorknobs that do not have the protection of a doorstop and on walls in eating areas against which a chair was often pushed back and made a dent. Repair the holes in the wallboard and then install a new doorstop.

Use wallboard compound to fill in nail holes. For larger holes in the wall, the process is a little more involved. Cut out the damaged area, use a wallboard patch to fill it in, apply wallboard compound, let it dry, and then sand smoothly. The repair costs are less than $20, and a doorstop that screws into the floor molding costs about $2, an inexpensive upgrade.

TIP: To patch holes or sags in plaster walls, use plaster washers, metal disks designed to secure the surface to the lath behind it.

If there are nail pops, crescent-shaped cracks caused by wallboard pulling away from warped wall studs, you can repair them. Use a nail set to drive the nail tight against the stud and then place a new nail a few inches above the original. Drive the new nail head into the wallboard far enough to hide the nail head and make a slight dimple in the wallboard. Fill the dimple above the nail head with wallboard compound, let it dry, and then sand smooth.

TIP: If you're choosing wallpaper and you want to make a room appear larger, choose a paper with a light background or horizontal stripes or pattern. In a small room, choose a small print. And to make a ceiling look higher, use a vertical stripe or pattern.

Closet Doors

Tune up closet sliding doors so that they open and close easily. Lift up the door so that its glide wheel comes off the track. Then inspect the rollers along the top; if they don't turn freely, apply a few drops of household oil. If the ball bearings don't move and the glide wheels are frozen, replace the tracks or glides, each $2 items.

Tune up bifold doors by cleaning the track installed on the top of the doorjamb. Lubricate the track with a silicone spray so that the doors will slide freely. Check that the doorstops on the floor are not bent, loose, or dirty. Replacement guides and hardware are sold in the hardware section of hardware stores and home centers, where you'll find a complete set of bifold-closet-door hardware for $18, a small investment to make the doors operational.

TIP: To clean the slats of louvered doors, first run a vacuum's crevice tool over the surface, especially in the corners to remove heavy dirt. Then wipe them with a dampened disposable foam paintbrush.

Add lighting to a closet without wiring by using battery-operated closet lights. Some of these $10 push on/off fixtures have a hanger for a clothes rack; others are installed on the wall with a backing of a self-stick adhesive.

TIP: To remove heavy furniture dents in carpeting, wet the dented area with a clean white rag and then use a hair dryer and a spoon or fork to gently lift the carpet fibers. For deep craters in the carpet fibers, you may need to repeat this process a few times.

Exterior Door

Add a sense of security by replacing an old lock with a new deadbolt lock for about $95. If you're giving your entry door a face-lift, replace the threshold, too, especially if you plan to change the carpeting or flooring material. If you discover, after removing layers of old flooring, that the surfaces are uneven, choose a threshold that is self-adjusting so that you can even out the surface. The best time to make these improvements is after you paint or finish the door.

TIP: Replace worn weather stripping around an exterior door with new material for an instant upgrade.

Storm/Screen Door

Make an old storm door look new with a $20 screen door handle. The job involves removing the old handle and checking the holes to see if they can be used for the new handle. If not, use the paper template that comes packaged with the handle as a guide for drilling new mounting holes.

If the pneumatic door closer binds or doesn't operate properly, clean the shaft with an oily rag to remove dirt or rust. Apply a light coating of lithium, also called white grease, to prevent rust and lubricate the seal. Adjust the screw in the end of the piston assembly to make the door close slower or faster. If the closer is too old to adjust, you can replace it with a new one in a few simple steps.

Sliding Patio Door

A patio door may be difficult to open and close because of a buildup of dirt or debris in the track that clogs the lubrication in the rollers. Clean out the track with cotton swabs; if that doesn't help, replace the old rollers with new track hardware, which costs about $15. You have to remove the door panels, so schedule the job during temperate weather.

Double-Hung Windows

If an old window sash is difficult to slide up and down, free up a stuck pulley with a squirt of WD-40 and then lubricate the pulley shafts with a squirt of 3-In-One oil. The pulleys are located at the top of the window jamb where the rope enters the jamb. The lower sash must be closed to expose the pulleys, but the upper sash has to be open to get to them. Use the extension straw of the can to direct the oil into the center of the pulley. The oil helps the wheels turn freely so that the window sash can open and close.

Window Glass

You can replace a windowpane in a double-hung window for about $20, which covers the materials. The job involves removing the broken pane and putty and then using new glazing putty and glazier points to secure the replacement glass.

Screens

Anyone can replace old or torn screening with new fiberglass screening fabric. First remove the spline in the groove of the frame that holds the screening in place. Then replace the screening and secure it with the old spline. If the spline is brittle, you'll need a roll of new spline. Fifteen dollars will buy the material and tools you need.

Windowsills

Two-part epoxy wood filler does a good job of rebuilding damaged wood and lets you shape and sand the surface so that it conforms to its original appearance. It's a good choice for fixing a rotten windowsill. The filler system has two parts: a liquid that's squeezed into the damaged sill to stabilize the wood, and a pastelike filler applied with a putty knife that hardens and conforms to the shape. When the filler is dry, you sand it smooth, and paint it.

Bathroom

Although it's a small room, a bathroom can be dirty, with a buildup of scum and mildew. It takes time and patience to scrub and scour, but your work will pay off because a dirty bathroom is a definite turnoff to home buyers.

TIP: A space-saver shelf unit that fits over a toilet in a small bathroom goes a long way to provide storage while giving a fresh, new look to the room.

Clean Surfaces

To remove the buildup of soap scum and watermarks on chrome bathtub fixtures, use a 50-50 solution of household vinegar and water. Soak a rag in the solution and wrap it around the fixture for a few minutes. Then use the rag to scrub the fixture. You may have to make more than one application for tough stains.

Use a spray cleaner that attacks mildew on all surfaces in the bathroom where mildew has grown. Increase the ventilation in the room to prevent mildew from returning.

Tile Grout

Apply a new coat of grout around a ceramic tile bathtub surround for a fast face-lift. It's a good idea to protect the tub floor with a heavy drop cloth or cardboard and remove the tub spout and handle faucets first. The job involves removing the old grout with an inexpensive grout saw, cleaning out the seams with the crevice tool of a vacuum, and then applying the new grout. Smooth the joints, wipe away the grout haze, caulk the joints, and then reinstall the fixtures.

TIP: If you're using a wrench or pliers on a faucet, wrap tape around the jaws to protect the finish on the faucet.

Bathtub Caulk

Remove old caulk with a putty knife and clean the joint between the wall and the tub and the wall around the sink. Scrub the joint with an old toothbrush to remove dirt and grit. Let the joint dry completely before applying a new silicone sealant or tub caulk, both of which are easy to apply.

TIP: Invest in two basic tools to keep sink drains running free and unclogged: a plunger and a snake, sometimes called a hand auger.

Kitchen

Even if Martha Stewart lived in your home's kitchen (which she probably didn't), go through the cabinets and appliances and scrub and scour them clean. This grunt work will pay off because no one wants to think about moving into a less-than-sparkling kitchen. Troubleshoot the appliances to make sure they're in working order.

Cabinets

Wash the insides of cabinets with a household cleaner. If cabinet pulls or hardware are worn or outdated, replace them with new hardware. To avoid having to drill new holes for new hardware and filling the old holes, bring a sample of the old hardware to the store. Limit your selection of new hardware to items with installation holes spaced like the old ones.

TIP: To rejuvenate dull brass hardware, use this solution: mix 1 tablespoon salt and 1 tablespoon household vinegar in 1 cup of hot water. Let the hardware soak in the solution for about 10 minutes, then use a soft brush or fine steel wool to rub the surface and dissolve the corrosion. Wash the hardware in soapy water, rinse and dry it, and then apply a brass polish to protect it.

Cabinet Hinges

Stuffing a wooden matchstick or toothpick into the screw hole with wood glue is one way to repair ill-fitting hinges, but that's a temporary fix. For a permanent repair, remove the loose screws and hinges and fill the holes with an epoxy or polyester wood filler mixed with its catalyst. After the filler has hardened, sand it and drill new screw holes to reinstall the hinge.

TIP: Add inexpensive under-cabinet lighting to a kitchen to improve its function and style. The low-profile fixtures come in strips that you can install easily in the shallow recess on the bottom of cabinets, and they plug into a wall receptacle.

Range Hood

Turn off the power to the range hood, or to the range if the hood is part of the appliance. Look for the grease filter, which is usually under the hood in front of the blower air intake. Remove the filter and wash it in soapy water. You may need a strong grease-cutting cleaner if the filter hasn't been cleaned recently. Use a scrub brush to remove grease and dirt between the grill louvers, and clean the inside of the fan housing and the exterior and interior of the hood. When dry, reassemble the filter and restore power.

TIP: To remove grease spots behind the stove, let steam from a water kettle on the back burner help. Let the walls become moist, wipe the area with a good household cleaner, and then rinse with clean water.

Dishwasher

Check to see that the pump screen and spray armholes are free of small food particles and mineral deposits. The pump screen is usually located in the well at the base of the unit. Scrub the screen with a stuff brush and soapy water. Use a straight pin or thin wire to unclog any holes you can't see through in the spray arm. Clean the exterior of the dishwasher.

Refrigerator

Clean the interior and exterior of the unit with soapy water and then pull it away from the wall so that you have access to the condenser coils located on the bottom or back. A buildup of dust and lint prevents the flow of air from inside the unit to the air outside. Use a long-handled snowbrush (from your car) to dust off the coils. If the refrigerator has a drain pan at the bottom, clean it thoroughly to remove odors.

Butcher Block

To renew a stained or knife-scarred butcher block, use a hook-type paint scraper with a sharpened blade and an electric palm sander. Protect the surface around the butcher block with a strip of masking tape. Then, following the grain of the wood, press down as you pull the scraper toward you. Use a palm sander with heavy sandpaper to work on dark stains or burn marks, then use light sandpaper to finish-sand the surface. Brighten the surface with a sponge and a 50-50 solution of household bleach and water. Then neutralize the bleach with a rag soaked in white vinegar and wash the surface with soap and water. Finally, sand the surface with lightweight sandpaper and apply a top finish with a clean rag soaked in mineral oil.

Safety and Efficient Systems

The safety of a house and the efficiency of its systems are important features noted by appraisers, home inspectors, and prospective buyers. Take the time to install the necessary safety equipment and service the systems so that the house makes a good impression.

Smoke and CO Detectors

This $30 device measures the concentration of CO (carbon monoxide) and smoke and sounds an alarm when a potentially harmful level is reached. Because the unit is battery-operated, there's no electric outlet needed. Install one alarm on each level of the house and outside the bedrooms. These detectors are on the list of requirements for insurance, so make sure they're installed when the house is inspected. Home inspectors look for them, too. Note that some CO detectors have sensors that must be replaced every couple of years. Be sure to leave the owner's manual for the new owners so they understand what is required to maintain the units.

Heat Pump or Central Air

Trim back any overgrown plants or shrubbery around the unit. While the foliage can shield the unit from the hot sun and make it more efficient, overgrown bushes can get sucked against the air-intake grill and block the flow of air through the coils.

Furnace

Use the crevice tool of a shop vacuum to clean the area around the blower of the furnace. Measure the size of the furnace filter and buy a new one to replace it.

TIP: Replace the filter once a month or as frequently as suggested by the manufacturer.

Radiators

Before the heating season begins, slowly empty or "bleed" the air from the system. Get a small can or bucket to catch the water runoff, and use a radiator key or screwdriver to turn the bleed valve stem counterclockwise about a half-turn or until you hear air hiss out. The bleed valve is located at the top end of the radiator and at one end of the baseboard convector. You may have to remove a cover or open the panel at the end of a baseboard unit to find the valve.

House Exterior

It's easy to forget about the exterior of a house unless you inspect it regularly. Make a favorable impression on everyone who drives by performing these basic maintenance chores for the outside of the house.

Gutters and Downspouts

Clean out gutters so that rainwater can drain through them and not pool around the foundation of the house. Position a diverter, also called a splash block (about $6 to $10), at the base of each downspout to direct the water away from the house. Seal any leaking joints with silicone caulk. Refasten any hangers and gutters that sag or have pulled away from where they are attached to the house.

TIP: Flush out clogged debris in downspouts with a garden hose by holding it at the top and turning on the hose full blast to remove any blockage.

Exterior Light and House Numbers

Drive up to the house in the evening when it is dark and see if you can read the address and if the front entry is well lighted. If not, replace the light and get larger house numbers.

Dirty Deck

Sweep the deck and hose it down with the spray nozzle of a garden hose. Then use a scrub brush broom to remove a buildup of dirt. Or rent a power washer to spray-wash the dirty deck. When the deck is clean and dry, apply a coat of sealer and repair any loose or broken boards, railing, or stairs. Rake out debris that accumulates beneath the deck.

TIP: If you're cleaning a deck or siding with a power washer, protect foundation plants nearby, especially if you're using a detergent. Lightly tie a rope around a tarp or plastic sheeting over the plants, and remove it as soon as your work is completed.

TIP: If you're repairing the deck, rent or buy a power screw gun that has plenty of screwdriving power for loose planks.

Brick Efflorescence

Sometimes brick develops a condition called efflorescence, in which mineral salts contained in the brick react with water in the masonry and rise to the surface and evaporate, leaving white blotches that look like dusting powder. To remove this, use a stiff wire brush and a garden hose to wash the surface. Then apply a coat of clear water sealer when the brick is clean and dry.

Find the cause of the excess moisture behind the brick and fix it. It might be a leaking gutter, a loose downspout, or missing caulk around doors and windows that lets water seep behind the brick.

Garage

Clean out the garage and organize anything that's stored there. If the previous owner left lawn tools behind, keep only the ones that are in good condition; get rid of everything else in the garage. Sweep the floor and scrub it with a heavy-duty degreaser. If there's a garage door opener, get fresh batteries for the remote opener and change the light-bulb in the garage.

Blacktop Driveway

If the driveway shows signs of wear, a new topcoat of sealer will improve its appearance, plus maintain it for longer use. Pull any weeds growing alongside the driveway and rake the area so that it is neatly edged. Before applying the sealer, sweep the surface and fill in any holes with an asphalt patching compound. Apply the sealer with an old push broom or applicator, spreading it from the garage door and working your way out toward the street. Don't forget to barricade the wet surface and park your car somewhere else while the coating dries.

Landscaping

Second only to putting a new coat of paint on the siding, trimming overgrown and neglected landscaping is an improvement that won't go unnoticed. With a few basic pruning and grooming lawn tools and a lawn mower, you can transform an eyesore into a nicely manicured landscape.

Lawn, Trees, and Shrubs

Maintain the lawn by cutting it on a regular basis. Prune and groom trees and shrubbery by cutting away the excess foliage, dried ends, and heavy branches with pruning shears and loppers. Get advice from a local lawn and garden center about the best time to prune specific trees and shrubbery in your area.

TIP: Schedule weed pulling after a rainfall when the soil is moist so that it's easier to remove all those unwanted plants. And plan to rake leaves when conditions are dry because wet leaves are heavy to lift and remove.

Edging Lawn and Garden Beds

A $20 edging tool and your time pays back with a neatly manicured lawn and garden beds. This is a no-brainer spruce-up that keeps the lawn from invading garden beds. Dig the edger down about six inches into the soil and create a V-shaped trench between the lawn and the garden. As you work, remove any weeds and loosen the soil so that it's easy to work with.

TIP: If you have a lot of yard work and landscaping tools and materials, use an inexpensive kid's plastic snow sled to drag it around the yard. Even heavy bags of mulch are easy to move this way. An old plastic wading pool is another good way to haul debris or materials in a yard.

Worn Lawn

Reviving a lawn involves removing the weeds, raking and leveling the soil, and adding materials such as organic matter, fertilizer, lime, or sulfur. Then apply a starter fertilizer and seed and nurture the new seedlings with a steady watering routine.

CHAPTER 14

SPACE-EXPANDING POSSIBILITIES

The areas of a house that are under the roof offer the best potential for expansion because they are already part of the structure.
An attic has an existing roof and floor, a basement is enclosed by the
existing structure, and a back or side porch is an unfinished annex just
waiting to be enclosed. Improving these spaces doesn't require expensive new foundation work or building exterior walls; instead, it's a matter of reusing the space to its optimum advantage. Therein lies the
challenge: knowing when a room offers untapped potential living space
and when it should be left as it is.

Of course, there are limiting factors to consider. No matter how
large an attic is, its joists and framing might not be constructed to withstand the load of additional living space; that basement may be plagued
with dampness. And an open porch, while tempting to enclose and convert, might add more architectural character and value to the house than
an enclosed space would. In this chapter, we'll look at how to recognize
expansion possibilities in the attic, basement, and porch and when and
how to tap their potential.

Converting an Unfinished Attic

Converting an unfinished attic takes advantage of the existing foundation, walls, roof, and siding. Finishing the space requires the basic car-

pentry skills of framing, insulating, and hanging wallboard and trim. To assess an attic, the first thing we look for is what we call an "easy convert," or a wide-open unfinished space that can be transformed into rooms. The addition of bedrooms and a bathroom can change a two-bedroom, one-bath house to a house with four bedrooms and two baths—a dramatic upgrade. The next best possibility is to convert an attic to usable, accessible storage space, a feature that's on every homeowner or renter's wish list.

Many 1920s-vintage bungalow- and Cape Cod-style homes were built with unfinished attics to attract budget-strapped homeowners who could finish the attic when their time and bank accounts allowed. These one-story homes typically have steep roofs framed with rafters and ceiling joists and were designed with a living room, dining room, kitchen, bathroom, two or three bedrooms, and a stairway leading to an unfinished attic. That stairway and unfinished attic offer a tremendous opportunity to upgrade the house.

LESSONS LEARNED

If the house has a low-pitch roof like a ranch or an attic with crisscrossing two-by-fours, which indicate that the roof has truss construction, forget about expansion possibilities because these attics are not designed to be used as living space.

Attic Inspection

You can make a general inspection of the attic at the same time you inspect it for conversion possibilities. Bring a flashlight, a 25-foot measuring tape, and a clipboard with paper on which make a rough sketch of the space and jot down your findings. Begin by looking at the attic ceiling or sheathing, which is actually the underside of the roof. Look for signs of any sagging areas or damage from insects, rot, or condensation. Pay particular attention to roof penetrations like the plumbing vent and the chimney, where leaks may occur. Sometimes what looks like water damage is actually condensation caused by inadequate ventilation. Look for vents and see if they are screened to deter animals from entering.

Depending on your geographic location, there are specific government recommendations and local building code requirements for the R value—the insulating power—of roof and wall insulation. In the past, 6 inches of attic insulation was considered enough, but in most parts of the country today, 12 inches is considered the minimum.

If there are recessed lighting fixtures in the ceilings of rooms below the attic, inspect the fixtures. First, go downstairs and look at the fixture in each room to find out its rating. An IC-rated fixture can be completely covered with insulation, but a non-IC- or T-rated recessed fixture must be at least three inches away from insulation. Also look for bathroom vents to see if they go to the outside. Look at the electric wiring to see that it is not damaged or spliced.

For expansion possibilities, look beyond the basics.

Access

The location of the stairs is a prime factor that determines whether an attic has living space potential. For aesthetics, the best location for a stairway is in the center of the house or off the main living or dining area, not tucked away at the back of the house. A centrally placed stairway provides easy access from the main living area.

The location of the stairway also determines the floor plan of the attic makeover. The best layout usually includes a central hall and landing from which there is access to all the rooms. There's nothing worse than tandem rooms lined up one after the other like railroad cars. A hall with doors leading to bedrooms and bathroom makes all the rooms on the second floor accessible and private so that no one has to go through one room to get to another one.

Yes, it's possible to relocate back stairs to another part of the first floor, but that's an expensive option that requires major structural changes. Instead, keep the stairs at the back of the house and use the attic as a storage area. The exception here is if the home is grossly undervalued for its neighborhood. In that case, totally redesigning the floor plan and moving the stairs might make sense.

In many homes, the staircase leading to an unfinished attic separates the dining room and kitchen and opens into the kitchen. In that case, you can open up the stairway and reroute the stairs so that they open into the dining room instead, making the staircase more formal and making it appear to have always been there. Close off the doorway to the stairs in the kitchen and gain more wall space there. Open the wall in the dining room and create a raised landing finished with a balustrade and woodwork that match the existing moldings and trim. This detail enhances the entire house and ties the staircase into the design of the home.

Building codes require that stair treads must be a minimum of 10 inches and stair risers a maximum of $7^3/4$ inches. The headroom must be no less than 80 inches, measured vertically from the finished floor at the landings.

The codes also require a second stairway or window as a means of escape. To meet this requirement, an egress/rescue window should be included in the plan for the conversion. This type of window, which allows for a convenient exit in the event of a fire, must have a minimum opening of at least 20 inches wide by 24 inches high, have a maximum sill height of 44 inches, and be operated without keys or tools. When installed at the correct height above the floor, some roof windows meet these requirements.

Floor Joists

Attics that were not designed for future conversions may have floor joists (actually the ceiling joists of the rooms below) that are too small to support a living area. Depending on the size of the rooms below, the attic floor joists must be at least two-by-six and possibly larger. Large rooms require larger floor joists because they must span long distances without additional support. Generally, if the attic floor has two-by-six or larger joists and the span between the load-bearing walls on the floor below does not exceed 10 to 12 feet, the floor is strong enough to support a living area, and we consider the space a candidate for remodeling.

Ask the local building department or a contractor or refer to a building codebook to determine the load factor. To support only the ceiling, the load is 10 pounds per square foot of the rooms below. For attic storage, the load is 20 pounds per square foot, and for a live load of people and furniture, the load is 30 to 40 pounds per square foot.

Building codes involving attic conversions are precise about joist size as it relates to the space between load-bearing walls. Before applying for a building permit, find out what the requirements are so that you can be sure that your plan will comply. In some cases the building department will require an engineer-architect to draw up and stamp the plan.

Headroom

We have found that a house with good access to a second floor and adequate headroom in the attic was built to support future expansion. The International Residential Code for one- and two-story dwellings requires that all habitable rooms, except bathrooms and kitchens, be no less than seven feet high. Some codes require $7^1/_2$ feet.

This underscores the importance of learning the requirements from the building department in the town or jurisdiction where a house is located. In some cases, sloped and flat ceilings lower than seven feet high are allowed, but the floor spaces under the portions that are lower than five feet aren't considered in the calculation of minimum room size.

When measuring the height of the attic space, keep in mind that you have to allow for furring strips, insulation, and wallboard to finish the ceiling and walls.

Fire Blocking

To contain the spread of fire through a concealed draft opening, a fire barrier between floors is required. Approved unfaced fiberglass insulation and lumber are used to fill any gaps between a chimney and the floor and ceiling as part of the framing stage of construction. These materials should be factored into the equation.

Lighting, Heating/Cooling, and Ventilation

When assessing an attic for conversion, don't forget to consider lighting the space and providing adequate temperature control and ventilation. Skylights and roof windows are obvious solutions. Consider tapping into the existing heating and cooling systems and adding ventilation, especially if a bathroom is part of the redesign. Thinking of all these considerations at the first inspection and appraisal will help you create comfortable and valuable living space.

Strictly-for-Storage Attics

Sometimes the only access to an attic is through a small panel in the ceiling, and this is often tucked away in a closet; if that's the case, the attic is guaranteed not to be designed for living space. You can replace the panel with a foldaway staircase, which is a more user-friendly way to access the attic for storing items. These staircase units, which are sold at lumberyards and home centers, come in a range of ceiling heights from 8 to 10 feet. The stairway is bolted into a rough opening and then trimmed with molding and painted to give a finished look to the ceiling. The heavier the unit, the better.

A carpenter will charge about $550 to install a good-quality foldaway staircase, so it's a sizable investment. But don't underestimate the value of storage space in a home. If other houses in the same neighborhood or price range have accessible storage space, adding foldaway stairs to untapped storage space is worth considering.

If you decide to add a staircase unit, rethink its location. It doesn't have to be where the small panel is located. Get a contractor to inspect the attic and its ceiling joists and suggest the best location for one. Ideally, the stairs will unfold into a room or hallway and be easily accessible to anyone using it.

Use the worksheet in Figure 14.1 to take notes when inspecting an attic, and review them when you're making a decision about whether to expand it.

LESSONS LEARNED

In an attic without flooring, the storage space is limited to balancing boxes and items across the span of the floor joists. To upgrade the storage capability, consider adding plywood sheets or tongue-and-groove panels laid over the floor joists and secured with wood screws.

Figure 14.1 Attic Worksheet

NOTES

Stairs

Width of steps _____

Headroom in stairway _____

Open or enclosed _____

Location in house _____

Adjoining walls _____

Location in attic _____

Headroom

At the roof peak or highest dimension _____

At the lowest sidewall _____

Floor Plan of Living Space

Length and width of floor space _____

Length and width of floor space with
    five feet of headroom _____

Dimensions of Floor Joists

Length and width _____

Insulation

Type and R-value (if any) in ceiling _____

Type and R-value or depth (if any)
    in floor _____

Insulation around recessed can
    light fixtures _____

Location of Permanent Fixtures

Chimney _____

Electric wires _____

Plumbing lines _____

NOTES

Heating ducts	_____
Built-ins	_____
Other things	_____

Flooring

Open, no finished floor	_____
Plywood sheathing or planks	_____

Attic Ceiling or Sheathing

Rafters	_____
Sagging areas	_____
Signs of pest infestation or rot	_____
Moisture or condensation, fungus	_____
Vents	_____

If the opening to the attic is narrow, cut the four- by eight-foot plywood sheets in half vertically so that they measure two by eight feet and will fit through the opening. Or use StorageBords, which are two- by four-foot panels. For less than $100, you can buy the panels for an eight-foot-square area and improve the storage space considerably.

Basement Conversions

You can take advantage of what a basement has to offer—walls, ceiling, and a floor—and transform it into usable living space. For an investor, it is wise to just create the finished space rather than dividing it into rooms for specific functions. Let the owner customize it; you just provide a clean, finished space that is very appealing to a buyer. If the furnace and other utilities and laundry facilities are there, separate them from the finished space with a partition wall, but don't do anything more than that.

Improvements that increase living space add value to the property. We always clean up the basement and sometimes remodel it. In the case of a small house, we feel that the additional living space can return more value than it costs. But this holds true only if the costs are carefully controlled. Creating a fancy basement family room will not pay off, but transforming a dingy basement into a clean, attractive, usable area will.

Basement Inspection

When you are considering finishing a basement, make an inspection to determine if it's suitable. Look at the foundation and walls for signs of seepage through small cracks, or a white powdery residue called efflorescence, or indications of mold or mildew. All of these telltale signs indicate that more than paint is needed. The fix might be as easy as cleaning the gutters so that rainwater can flow through them and adding a downspout diverter to direct it away from the foundation. Also, inspect several areas of the cement floor for cracks and signs of moisture. If you find chronic signs of moisture or cracks and crevices, call in a waterproofing specialist for a diagnosis.

Stairwells and Windows

If there is an exterior stairwell with concrete stairs, look to see if they are solid or cracked. If there's a drain, does it work? Window wells should be free of water and debris, and the basement windows should open easily and not show signs of wood rot.

Electric Wiring

Look at the electric wiring. It should be grounded and show no signs of damage or splices. Be concerned about wires that go nowhere. Basements should have three-prong and GFCI receptacles. These provide shock protection at electric receptacles by cutting the power almost instantly when they detect a possible dangerous current imbalance. Also look at any lighting fixtures and find their switches.

Plumbing

Inspect the plumbing lines to see whether they are copper, plastic, or galvanized, and notice how the lines are connected and secured to ceiling rafters. Metal strapping should be tight and secure. Be sure to find the main water line and see if there is a shutoff valve or a check valve or an antibackflow device.

And look for the drain lines that take water out of the house. See how they are connected, and look for signs of leaks. Look at the sump pump and trip the float rod to test it. When you lift the rod, the motor should start.

Insect Problems

Look at the exposed joists in the ceiling for signs of rot or pest infestation. Termites are a potential problem in most parts of the United States. A professional termite inspection is required in many parts of the country in order to get financing.

Appraising a Basement for Living Space

To determine if a basement is suitable for living space, first look at two key issues: moisture and ceiling height.

Moisture

By their very nature, the concrete walls and floors that make up the foundation of a house draw moisture from the ground in varying degrees. Small amounts of moisture or condensation that forms on concrete walls can be managed with a dehumidifier. Two solutions for handling larger amounts of moisture are installing a sump pump cut into the floor or digging drainage ditches with gravel and installing drain lines around the high sides of the foundation. Don't consider any improvements to a basement without first removing sources of moisture. And give any property second thoughts if there are signs of serious water problems in the basement.

Ceiling Height

For a basement to be finished for living space, most building codes require the ceiling height to be at least 90 inches, which is $7^1/_2$ feet. Because most basements in older houses were not built with finishing in mind, heating ducts, plumbing lines, and electric wires were installed exposed so that they were easy to work on. When finishing the basement takes priority, the utilities must remain accessible and convenient for repair work but concealed for aesthetics.

Enter the suspended or drop ceiling, a solution for all seasons. A suspended ceiling consists of metal channels that run the length of a room, with cross runners and ribs that create a grid for two- by two-foot or two- by four-foot acoustical panels that slip into place. This type of ceiling is an ideal way to cover up utilities, yet provide access to them because, while the channels are permanently fastened to the ceiling joists, the panels are easily removed. Another component of a suspended ceiling system is recessed lighting, which illuminates the room with overall lighting without taking up valuable space overhead.

Another way to hide the web of utility lines and furnace ducts is by boxing them in with soffits made of wood framing covered with wallboard. An even easier way is to fool the eye and just paint them the same color as the ceiling and walls. Any of the service lines and pipes can be removed and rerouted in a basement ceiling, but it's extremely expensive. For investment purposes, consider only concealing them, not relocating them.

Basement for Storage

The best bang for the buck in a basement is cleaning it, emptying it, and painting it—period. A potential buyer can either envision how he or she will finish the room or see it as a ready-made storage area, and in either case, it's an appealing feature.

Use a shop vacuum to suck out dust and dirt, especially cobwebs hidden in the ceiling and behind heating ducts and plumbing pipes. Remove any and all debris that's left in the basement. Use a power washer to clean the walls and floor (if necessary).

Deal with any moisture issues by finding the source of the problem and making the necessary repair. Turn on a dehumidifier to remove the dampness.

Paint the walls with a good latex paint with a sprayer or roller. Use a good floor and porch paint to coat the floor, being careful to cut in the paint where the floor meets the bottom of the walls.

Walls and Support Poles

Wallboard, also called Sheetrock or gypsum board, is the best way to finish basement walls. Wallboard installed over concrete should have a barrier between the two to eliminate any condensation. Many contractors isolate damp concrete walls with one inch of extruded polystyrene insulation and a layer of six-mil polyethylene. This type of vapor barrier prevents trapped moisture behind the walls.

Dealing with stack pipes and support poles located in the center of a basement can be a challenge. You can't remove them, but you can conceal them. A low-budget solution is to camouflage them with a rope wrap to soften their appearance. Choose a thick natural rope or braided boat dock line, wrap it around the pole, and glue it, beginning at the bottom and working to the top. A more costly but attractive solution is to conceal a support pole as a column, an architectural feature of the room. Have a carpenter build a column around it, with collar blocks to anchor and support side panels made of plywood. Trim the top and bottom with molding, and paint it to match the walls.

Floors and Stairs

To create a floating laminate floor system that is built up and not directly attached to the slab, some contractors suggest using polyethylene rigid-foam insulation over one-by-three sleepers and tongue-and-groove plywood. However, this raises the floor, which can lead to problems with an already low ceiling or create an issue with the distance between the floor and the first stair riser. We usually use carpeting with a good pad underneath it.

A staircase should have a sturdy handrail secured to a wall and provide safe footing. There should be a gap of five inches or less between vertical balusters and the stair treads, and risers should be safe and well built, whether they are open or closed.

Most building codes call for a minimum of $7^3/4$ inches for stair risers and 10 inches for treads. We've had the best luck with carpeting enclosed stairs and painting open wooden stairs.

Windows

Windows in basements let daylight in, but at the same time they can create a security breach if the glass can be broken. Consider replacing any old windows with basement hopper windows with either double-pane insulating glass or double-insulated acrylic block panels.

If there is no outside exit from a basement, an egress window—that is, one that is large enough to allow a person to get out in case of an emergency—is often required. Some older homes were built before there were any egress window requirements, so ask the building inspector about the code.

Climate Control

Talk to an HVAC (heating, ventilation, and air conditioning) contractor to find out if the existing heating, ventilating, and air-conditioning system can be used in the basement. The contractor can tell if the system can handle the additional square footage or if an additional system will be needed. Most basements are easy to heat and usually have some ducts already installed. The pipes running through the basement from the hot-water-heating system usually provide adequate heat for the space there. Don't enlarge a well-functioning heating or cooling system just to accommodate the basement. But if the system requires upgrading anyway, consider upsizing it to accommodate the basement.

LESSONS LEARNED

You know the story about the guy who built the boat in his basement and couldn't get it out? Well, the reverse of that is getting cumbersome building materials inside. Spend time mapping out a strategy to schedule the arrival and delivery of materials, especially bulky ones like wallboard and carpeting.

Use the worksheet in Figure 14.2 to take notes when inspecting a basement, and review them when you're making a decision to expand it.

Figure 14.2 Basement Worksheet

NOTES

Exterior Stairwells

Drain _____

Cracked stairs _____

Window wells

Free of water and debris _____

Foundation and Walls

Signs of seepage through small cracks _____

Efflorescence or a white powdery
   residue _____

Mold or mildew _____

Interior Stairs

Handrail secured to a wall _____

Five-inch or less gap between vertical
   balusters _____

Open or closed stair treads and risers _____

Floor

Cracks in cement floor or slab _____

Sump Pump

Free of water and debris _____

Test by pulling up the float rod _____

Ceiling Joists

Signs of rot or pest infestation _____

NOTES

Electrical Wiring

Wires that go nowhere   _____

Spliced or damaged wires   _____

Grounded wires   _____

GFCIs   _____

Grounded outlets   _____

Lighting Fixtures

Location and switches   _____

Plumbing Lines

Type of water lines (copper, plastic, galvanized)   _____

How the lines are connected   _____

How the lines are secured to ceiling rafters (metal strapping)   _____

Main Water Line

Location   _____

Shut-off valve   _____

Check valve or anti-backflow device   _____

Drain Lines

Locations   _____

How they are connected   _____

Signs of leaks   _____

Enclosing a Porch

In older homes, many porches were designed to provide an extra outdoor space for use during warm weather in the northern climates and during the cool, breezy season in the South. The porch was a temporary room, sometimes enclosed with screens or windows, often with an open portico to catch the breeze and provide a shaded retreat from the sun. Over the years, many porches have been reincarnated as permanent rooms because they can be easily converted. The key, however, is knowing when to reinvent a porch as part of the house and when to leave it as it was intended. Most porches on older homes were built to lighter specifications than the structure they are attached to. While you can modify them to meet current building codes, you have to weigh the additional expense against the payback for that investment.

Just because a porch can be converted into permanent living space doesn't mean that it should be. There has been many a "remuddling" of charming old Victorian houses where the owner enclosed the front porch. Yes, it adds warm living space to the front of the house, but it destroys the value of the architecture and consequently reduces the value of the house.

However, the side and back porches of a Dutch Colonial or farmhouse are good candidates for conversion to living space. Often these porches were built on the side or rear of the house, usually with entry from the kitchen. The porch had three exterior walls with large screen windows and walls trimmed in bead board as wainscoting. The wall between the interior and the porch was often finished with the exterior siding. The porch was covered by the roof, which extended over and enclosed it.

Conversion Possibilities

The location of the porch is the first thing that determines its potential use. For example, the floor plan for a kitchen can be enhanced if there is an adjacent back porch because it provides expansion space for an eat-in kitchen or a kitchen and family room. A side porch off a living or dining room makes a convenient location for a den or library or playroom. Converting a porch usually involves insulating the walls and ceiling, adding or upgrading the windows, adding heat and electricity, and finishing the interior with wallboard, flooring, and woodwork.

Investigating a Porch Down Under

Before you make any decision about converting a porch to year-round living space, do some investigation work to appraise its construction and condition. Get a flashlight, a measuring tape, and a clipboard with notepad and poke around underneath the porch to see what's down there. If you have knee pads, wear them. Make a sketch and take measurements of the length and width of the four sides and the height of the walls to see how high the porch is off the ground.

Floor Joists and Beams

Look at the size and direction of the floor joists and the spans of the main beams, which bear the full load of the floor joists. Code specifications will vary according to the size of the porch, but two-by-six floor joists on 16-inch centers should be considered a minimum requirement.

Footings

Inspect the footings and posts in the corners and along the sides that support the porch. Brick piers should have all mortar joints filled and show no signs of cracking.

Pest Damage

In the framing beneath the porch, look for signs of wood rot or damage from termites, carpenter ants, or beetles, any of which could require more extensive repair and replacement work. Of course a termite and pest inspection should be considered mandatory before you purchase the property.

Lines, Ducts, and Pipes

Find the electric lines, heating ducts, and plumbing pipes, and see how they are routed under or near the porch. If these utilities are near the porch, tapping into them is easier and less expensive. This is especially true if you want to tie into an existing forced-air heating/cooling system. Long duct runs are expensive to install, and they reduce the efficiency of the system.

Also inspect the basement or crawl space adjacent to the porch and note the location of these utilities before completing plans.

If, after giving the porch a going-over, you find that there are many problems and the porch needs repair, use this information as a bargaining chip when negotiating the price. The costs of extensive repairs are difficult to fully recover. For the property to be marketable, it must be in good repair. Have the cost of needed repairs reflected in a reduced purchase price; don't expect the repairs to greatly increase the value of the property.

Evaluating the Porch Interior

Measuring and appraising the interior of the porch is easier than crawling around on your hands and knees. Make a rough sketch of the interior, noting the length and width of the walls, the size of the windows, and the height of the ceiling.

If the porch will be a stand-alone room with the same entrance, like a den off a dining room, the conversion issues are straightforward. However, the conversion becomes a major project if the porch will become part of another room, like an eat-in kitchen, as this involves converting the space and making the transition to the existing house so that the porch appears to be part of the house and not an appendage to it. On the outside, the exterior siding on the porch should be aesthetically pleasing and match or blend with the existing siding. Windows, doors, and trim should be the same style as those of the house so that from outward appearance the porch is part of the house.

Inside, attention to detail makes the difference between a new space appearing to be tacked on or to be an integral part of the house. The transition can be achieved by using the same flooring material in the new space and duplicating the woodwork and trim from the existing house throughout the porch conversion.

Climate Control

Talk to an HVAC contractor about heating and air-conditioning a porch conversion. The pro will inspect the existing heating and cooling unit to see if it can be tapped into or if an auxiliary unit is needed. Many older houses that we remodeled had a furnace or boiler with the extra capacity to heat an enclosed porch because the unit was oversized to begin with. And the unit had even greater capacity after we upgraded the energy efficiency of the house by adding insulation and weather stripping. This may not be true for newer houses, which have furnaces with capacities carefully matched to the size of the house. In such cases, a heating contractor can advise you.

Windows and Siding

Most porch windows are old and not insulated, so replacing them is necessary. Look at the style and size of the windows throughout the house and choose new ones to match. Use siding that matches or blends with the existing siding to enhance the exterior.

Ceiling and Walls

Many porch ceilings and walls are clad in bead board and not insulated. In some, the interior wall is actually the exterior siding. Insulating the ceiling and three exterior walls will dramatically improve the space; framing, drywall, and woodwork will make it a room.

LESSONS LEARNED

We have found that baseboard radiant electric heat is probably the easiest heating system to install in a porch, although it is expensive to operate. But we couldn't use it every time we wanted to. Unlike furnaces, existing electric panels seldom have excess capacity. One house had an electric panel with only 100-ampere capacity, which allowed us to add a branch circuit for lighting and receptacles, but not for radiant electric heat (that usually requires 150 amperes). We installed baseboard hot-water heat instead, tapping into the existing hydronic system.

Floors

To create a natural transition from a porch to the house, we raise the porch floor level (if necessary) by building it up with sleepers and plywood sheeting. Then we finish the floor to match the adjoining room's floor (usually carpeting or hardwood) and use a low-level door threshold. We remove the door to the porch and the trim around the doorjamb, which widens the opening, then finish the space with wallboard.

Use the worksheet in Figure 14.3 to take notes when inspecting a porch, and review them when you're making a decision about whether to enclose it.

Figure 14.3 Porch Worksheet

NOTES

Access to Porch

Adjoining what room? _____

Width of door _____

Floor Plan of Interior Space

Length, width, and height _____

Walls and Ceiling

Cladding _____

Condition _____

Insulation _____

Windows

Sizes to remove _____

Sizes to replace _____

Flooring

Material _____

Condition _____

NOTES

Utilities

Electric receptacles   _____

Light fixtures   _____

Heating/cooling   _____

Foundation

Length, width, and depth   _____

Material   _____

Condition   _____

Floor Joists and Beams

Size and material   _____

Condition   _____

Covered with insulation   _____

Footings

Location and number   _____

Condition   _____

Utilities

Electric lines   _____

Heating ducts   _____

Plumbing pipes   _____

Ground

Condition of soil   _____

CHAPTER 15

WHO DOES THE WORK? WHO MANAGES THE JOB?

These two questions—who does the work and who manages the job—shouldn't be taken lightly because the answers are important to the success of a rehab project whether you resell, rent, or live in the property. The duration of the work and what it costs are the keys to a quick turnaround if you're investing to resell the property. The under-construction time may be even more important if the renovation is extensive and you're living in the house while it is being remodeled.

There are many work and management scenarios that investors devise, but for your first investment property, we caution you to be conservative in your estimates of time, projected costs, and skill level. In other words, don't quit your day job, buy a fixer-upper, and dive into the project without fully understanding the management skills and construction expertise that are needed.

Being physically fit isn't a prerequisite for rehabbing, but being in shape sure helps if you plan to do some or all of the work. You'll quickly learn that swinging a hammer and hanging wallboard are not jobs for the faint of heart. Hauling heavy materials, working on your hands and knees driving screws in a deck, and crouching underneath a sink fixing a leak are demanding physical jobs that require a lot more stamina than does working at a desk. Rehabbing gives you a good workout, not to mention a few aches and pains.

Multitasking: Wearing Many Hats on the Job

Planning the work schedule for a rehab property requires a different set of management skills from those needed for an office job. Granted, there are very few interoffice memos to digest and even fewer meaningless meetings to attend. But there are many high-level skills needed—making on-the-spot decisions, scheduling the work of subcontractors who have many other clients besides you, ordering the correct amount of materials, coping with work delays and interruptions because of weather, and dealing with building inspectors. The stress and hassles of business travel may soon be replaced by waiting for a plumber to arrive to complete a job before a scheduled inspection or rescheduling work because of a freak hailstorm. Giving a PowerPoint presentation might seem like a walk in the park compared with some of the day-to-day adjustments required for your house rehab.

Do All or Some or None of the Work

Your first decision is whether you should do all the rehab work from start to finish, subcontract some of the work to yourself, act as the general contractor and manage the project, or hire a general contractor to manage the project. Let's look at each of these possibilities.

You Do All the Work

If you're retired and have time on your hands, you are in an ideal situation to do all the work yourself, futzing around the property, working at your own speed, and enjoying the process. If you have a day job, don't quit it until you've first bought and sold a property on a part-time basis. Rehabbing a house for rent or resale is a full-time, short-term job that ends only when the property is sold or rented and the profit is in your pocket.

Hire Yourself as a Subcontractor

Another twist to this scenario is if you do some of the work, acting as a subcontractor who will complete some phase or phases of the work so that you don't have to pay someone else to do it. For example, the initial grunt work of removing old kitchen cabinets, flooring, or wallpaper is ideally suited for a handy property owner. You can pay the tradespeople to do installations and get in and get out without charging you for the tear-out work.

But be realistic about your time and talents. It will cost you money if you take on a phase of the work and then don't complete it. There's nothing worse than a no-show property owner who keeps hired workers from completing their jobs and consequently delays the workflow.

Another advantage of hiring yourself as a subcontractor is obvious—the saving in labor costs will flow to the bottom line. There's an additional benefit if the improvement funds come from a bank loan that includes labor costs. By paying yourself for the labor, you can create a cash flow during the rehab phase of the property. It doesn't matter who does the work to make improvements that add value to the property.

You Act as a General Contractor and Hire Subcontractors

If you're good at multitasking and can keep your day job to support you, consider acting as the general contractor. This role requires free time during the day every week, so if you work nights and are available during the day, it's an option to consider. During the day, you have to manage the job—make phone calls, check on the delivery of materials, find out if workers showed up, or schedule an appointment with a plumber or building inspector. Being the general contractor, you're responsible for managing and controlling the project, but you aren't required to do the actual work.

The challenge is managing the work of others when you're not on-site 24 hours a day, 7 days a week. Of course, cell phones have made this job easier, but it still requires management skills, like scheduling different jobs so that they mesh and don't overlap, and confronting workers who don't show up—or who do show up, but don't perform work that meets your expectations. If you can finesse the time during your day job and are good at making follow-up calls, working out contingency plans, and thinking on your feet, you'll make a good general contractor.

Here's where having a partnership with another investor works very well in rehabbing a house. Or if you're working and living in a rehab house, it helps if one partner is a stay-at-home worker. "Being there" is a key advantage.

Hire a General Contractor to Oversee the Project

Typically a general contractor charges 15 to 25 percent of the total cost of a project, so right off the bat, you have to add that expense to the cost of the job. However, if neither you nor a partner is able to be there to manage the project, it's money well spent because the longer a property lingers without improvements being made, the more money is eaten up on the loan side.

Finding a Good Contractor and Subcontractors

Have you ever been at a cocktail party where the hot topic of discussion is not politics or sports or movies—it's contractors? We've heard countless stories from friends, relatives, and total strangers about their experiences dealing with no-show contractors or their praise and admiration for the precision work of their tile installers. When you find a good contractor who is a joy to work with, rehabbing can be a pleasure. Our experience has been that we treat our contractors well and they usually treat us well.

Many contractors prefer working with investors to working with homeowners because investors know what they want done, they don't change their mind, and they can lead to more work and become steady customers if they continue to invest and rehab property on a regular basis. These traits are appealing to a specialty contractor who wants to get in and out of a job without a lot of hassles.

Developing a list of reliable contractors and specialty subcontractors takes time, but with each job you'll find those you like to work with. For a first-time investor looking for a contractor, there are two basic approaches. In the first, you do the search and find the contractor; in the second, you use a service to find the contractor.

You Do the Search

The best reference for a contractor that you can get comes from someone you know. Maybe it's another investor or a friend or a real estate
broker. The best choice is someone who has had work completed by a
contractor whom he or she would hire again. If you can take a look at
the work before calling the contractor, that's even better.

If you can't get a referral from a friend who recommends a contractor, check with a local building-supply dealer. Dealers will often recommend a contractor who is one of their customers. The last alternative
is to make cold calls to contractors listed in the Yellow Pages or advertising in a local newspaper.

Home-Center-Installed Sales and Design Services

Using the installation service from the retailer where you buy materials is another way to find a contractor. Most of the major retailers and
building-supply centers offer an "installed sale" price on their mer-
chandise. This includes big-ticket items such as roofing, siding, replacement windows, and heating and cooling systems as well as the most
popular installed materials like flooring, doors, window treatments,
water heaters, and all built-in appliances.

This is a turnkey service that's popular with consumers who don't
have the time to find, or can't find, references. It's also a solution for a
property investor because it eliminates the process of finding contractors. In most of these agreements, the retailers imply that they stand
behind the installation, which is something to ask about. The agreement should clarify the responsibilities of the customer, the contractor,
and the retailer.

If the kitchen or bathroom needs more than a cosmetic face-lift, the
design service at a home center can be a great help. Make an appointment with a design specialist, and bring accurate measurements (snap-
shots are helpful, too) of a kitchen or bathroom. You can work with the
specialist to choose materials and lay out the design of the room. Be up-
front about your budget, and the specialist will direct you to a design
using cabinets and appliances that fit that budget and will manage the

installation. Sometimes there's a design fee in the $100 range that is applied to the purchase of the materials. The service saves you a tremendous amount of time and anguish in maximizing your investment in these two important rooms.

Using an Online Contractor's Referral Service

Who would have thought that you could use the worldwide Internet to find a contractor in your neighborhood? Online referral businesses like www.servicemagic.com and www.improvenet.com are lead-generation services or networks that offer an alternative way to find a good contractor because they connect qualified customers with qualified contractors—a win-win situation for both parties. When contractors join and become a member of the network, they are prescreened and profiled by the service, ensuring that they have a clean legal and credit history, current insurance, and a license to practice. They pay for leads to new customers, typically anywhere from $10 for a plumbing repair to $50 for a bathroom remodeling project. Sometimes the contractor pays more if the lead turns into a sale. Some of these services are free for homeowners; others require an annual membership fee.

At the service's Web sites you'll be asked to enter a detailed description of the project so that the members of the network in your area can decide if they'd like to bid on the job. Your project description is e-mailed to the specialty contractor members who serve your location. Based on that and their availability, they respond to the service and then are referred to you.

First Impressions

If you use a retailer-installed sales service or an online referral service, a contractor will call you. If you do the search, you'll make the initial phone call to a short list of contractors and subcontractors you want to consider. Use your notebook to keep a record of whom you call and when. Make sure you have a succinct message so that when you're prompted to leave an answering machine message, you can quickly explain your reason for calling. Leave your phone number and the best time for you to receive calls. Explain your time frame and that your project is an investment property.

When you speak with contractors, find out if they are licensed and insured for workers' compensation, property damage, and personal liability. Ask a lot of questions: Do they like working on investment property? How many projects do they typically have going on at the same time? Do they work alone or have helpers? Ask about their availability.

Be able to clearly describe the project. For example, if you're talking to a painting contractor, you should know the approximate room sizes and the condition of the walls. A flooring installer will want to know the room size and how many layers of material are already on the floor. A roofer will ask if the roof is leaking and if there are multiple layers of shingles. Certainly you can't be expected to know everything before talking with a contractor, but you should know the basics of the work that's required.

Ask the contractor for the names of satisfied customers and call them. When you do, ask if you can see the contractor's work at their home. Usually people are willing to let you take a look, especially if they liked the contractor and think their cooperation will bring the contractor more work.

LESSONS LEARNED

We found that the best time to reach most contractors is first thing in the morning. They're usually on the road early with a cell phone in their ear, so they're available to talk with or you can leave a voice message.

A Good Contract: Putting It in Writing

The Remodelers Council of the National Association of Home Builders suggests what should be in a remodeling agreement. As a legal document, the contract between you and a contractor should spell out what, where, how, time span, and cost of your project. It should be clear, complete, and concise and should include the provisions that follow. When a contractor presents a contract to you to authorize work, make sure you understand the details before you sign it.

The Main Agreement

- Name the property owner and the contractor and their state or local jurisdiction license or registration number.
- List the address or legal description of the property found on the deed.
- Give a detailed description of the project.
- List all work to be done, including the specifications for the work and the contractor's warranty. To avoid confusion, this may also specify work that will not be done or that someone else will do.
- Include a visual representation, such as a floor plan, blueprint, or sketch, that illustrates what the contractor will do and where.
- Specify a project timetable that includes estimated start and completion dates. This may include language that stipulates conditions such as adverse weather that would require an extension of the completion date.
- Include a price and payment schedule that indicates how much you must pay at the start of the project, at specified intervals during the project, and at completion. The agreement should mention any deposits you may have already made.
- A predetermined bonus for early completion is sometimes included to provide an incentive for a contractor to finish the work ahead of schedule.
- Sometimes a liquidated damages clause is included that requires payment of a predetermined amount of money for breach of contract, such as an unreasonably late completion of the project or failure to pay subcontractors or material suppliers, and present necessary lien waivers.
- A section may stipulate a date by which you must sign the contract to obtain the price quoted.

All parties to the agreement must sign it. Each of you should retain a signed original for your records. When the agreement is signed, both you and the contractor should initial and receive a complete set of drawings, plans, and specifications.

General Conditions of a Contract

- The contract should include a section about who will obtain and pay for any necessary building permits and other approvals. It may also specify that the contractor agrees to comply with all applicable health and building codes, statutes, regulations, and ordinances governing the work and the way the contractor performs it.

- The contract usually lists the insurance that the project requires, including the contractor's policies covering employees, subcontractors, and the project, such as workers' compensation and liability insurance. It may also list any increase in homeowner's insurance that you will need to carry.

- A section should explain the possibility of unforeseeable conditions (such as rusty pipes behind a wall or under a floor) and provide a contingency in case these conditions increase the price of the job.

- The contract gives procedures to follow if hazardous materials— such as lead paint, radon, or asbestos—are encountered on the job site. You may agree in advance that you will hire specialty abatement contractors to remove the materials. This allows the contractor to suspend activity on the project until the appropriate specialty contractor takes care of the hazard.

- The people who work on or provide materials for a project are legally entitled to obtain a specific interest in or to place a lien on the property if you do not pay them. The contract should require that you receive a lien release (either partial or final, depending upon the type of payment) when you make payments to the contractor. By signing a lien release, your contractor and suppliers waive their rights to place a lien on your property.

- A contract should include a list of anyone other than the contractor and crew who will be working on your house. Even if the person working on it is you, the owner, this should be spelled out in the contract, assuring that the contractor is not responsible for that work and that he or she will not guarantee it.
- A change order is a written agreement to alter the work described in the original contract. It details how you can make changes after work has begun and protects the contractor from dealing with a series of revisions that could greatly alter the cost and completion date of the project. If there is payment required for a change order, it is stipulated. Figure 15.1 is a sample change order.

Working Conditions

A description of the working conditions and how the workers can affect those conditions may be handled in a separate form or during a preconstruction meeting rather than being included in the original agreement.

- *Access and working hours.* Your contract may indicate how workers can access the work site; restrict access to the work area by children, pets, and other unauthorized persons; and specify the working hours during which workers may be on the premises.
- *Care of the premises.* Any specific steps that you and the crew will take to preserve landscaping and protect rooms that are not being remodeled are specified.
- *Bathroom and phone.* Whether workers may have the use of your property's bathroom and telephone is specified; otherwise, the location for a portable toilet is decided.
- *Smoking, radios.* If workers are prohibited from smoking on the premises or playing a loud radio, that information will appear in the contract.
- *Cleanup and trash removal.* The responsibilities, schedules, and procedures for daily and final cleanup are specified, as is the extent of daily "broom clean" cleanup; also, the condition of the property when the job is completed should include specific information, such as "Dumpster removed," "all debris removed," and so on.

Figure 15.1 Change Order

Date: _____

Original date of contract: _____

Property address: _____

Property owner: _____

Contractor: _____

Change order number: _____

Request for Change Order

The undersigned owner and contractor agree to approve and perform work that is substantially different from the original scope of the project. Both parties know that the requested changes, which are listed below, may change the price and completion schedule. Any differences in the cost of the project relating to this change order will be taken into account for the regular payment schedule.

The contractor will perform the following work:

_____

_____

_____

_____

_____

_____

_____

_____

The total cost for labor and materials to be added or deducted: _____

How the change will affect the completion schedule: _____

New estimated completion date: _____

Contractor approval and date: _____
                                                        Signature

Owner approval and date: _____
                                                        Signature

_____

- *Personal property.* If someone is responsible for removing the property owner's tools or materials, it should be specified. And if items are to be saved from demolition, it should be noted where they should be stored.
- *Sign posting.* If a contractor wants to post his or her sign, that should be included in the contract, along with the size of the sign and the length of time it will be on the property.
- *Rescission right.* By law, all home-improvement contracts are required to give you three days to change your mind and cancel after signing.
- *Dispute resolution.* A clause should detail the terms of dispute resolution and arbitration procedures as a way to resolve a problem if it arises.

Warranty

If the contractor offers a warranty, a description of that warranty may appear in the contract or as a separate document referenced in the contract. The warranty will explain the responsibilities of the contractor regarding workmanship and materials. This document typically provides a limited guarantee that if the work on the project does not meet accepted industry practices, the contractor will make repairs or replacements or provide a refund as necessary. Many contractors will guarantee their workmanship for one year.

Checklist Before Signing a Contract

After reading a contract and asking any questions you have, read the document again. Does it include these items?

- Name, address, and business phone number of the contractor
- Start and finish dates
- Method, amount, and payment schedule
- Detailed written specifications of design and products
- A system to handle changes
- A description of your lien rights, dispute resolution, and the contractor's warranty
- A statement of a right to change your mind and cancel the contract within 72 hours

Timing and Money Disbursement

Contractors have their own policies about down payments and their preferred payment schedules. Many of them work on a three-part payment schedule that works like this: you pay one-third of the total price when signing the contract (down payment), another third when the work is half completed, and the final third when all the building inspections have been successfully completed and the house is ready to occupy. Often 10 percent of the total amount is held back as an incentive to the contractor for completing any last-minute work. In some arrangements the same scheduling is used, but on a quarterly basis.

If you're financing your project with a loan, make sure the loan-disbursement schedule is in sync with your contractor's billing intervals. For example, if the payment schedule for the contractor is February 1, the loan disbursement should have been received by the last week of January so that there is time for money to be deposited and checks issued.

Time and Materials for Services

Some subcontractors doing a specific job want to be paid on a time and materials basis, also called cost-plus. For example, a mason repairing a chimney might say that he can't accurately bid the job because he has to do some investigating before getting started. In that instance, he'll charge an hourly rate plus the cost of the new materials needed. We haven't been burned using this arrangement, but it makes it very difficult to calculate your expenses, since the costs are unknown.

Managing the Project

It really does not matter whether you are doing the project yourself, are acting as a general contractor, or have hired a contractor; you must be in control. Finding the right contractor or subcontractor and signing a well-written contract are just the first steps toward completion. Unless you are actively managing the project, things can and usually do go awry. This does not mean that you should micromanage the project, but you must stay on top of the project's progress and keep track of the costs.

Staying in Touch Is a Top Priority

If you're managing the job and working at the property or you have a partner who is doing so, staying in touch with contractor is easy. You're right there and available to make a decision or adjust your schedule if necessary. The challenge is keeping that line of communication open when you're at the office—or worse, out of town—and the workers are at the job site. Of course, cell phones have changed the way all of us communicate, but playing telephone tag can be frustrating for both the contractor and the investor, so we see a tremendous advantage in being on-site or having a partner who is.

To keep things on track, establish a weekly update meeting or walk-through. Friday is a good day to do a lot of things: review the progress for the week, make sure the next week's materials are on-site, and discuss any upcoming issues. You can ask what the workers are scheduled to complete the next week and if any materials or deliveries are expected. Being on-site is the best way to keep track, but if that's not possible, a weekly scheduled update can be made by phone or e-mail. The point is that as the property owner, you need to know that the various workers are coordinated so that the workflow continues without stopping.

Keeping Records

Whether you're doing the work, managing others, or hiring a general contractor to manage the property rehab, it's important for you to keep records—of everything.

- *Material samples and product information.* Use a box, a canvas sack, or a briefcase to keep product samples and brochures.
- *Price quotes and bid sheets.* Keep estimates for work and correspondence with suppliers and contractors in a pocket notebook.
- *Contact information.* Stay in touch with workers by having a readily available list of phone numbers and e-mail addresses. Keep the list on paper, a laptop, or a PDA (personal digital assistant).
- *Log sheet of phone calls.* This doesn't have to be detailed; just keep a record of the date and subject of your conversations with workers, suppliers, and brokers. It's a good way to keep track of your communications.

Controlling Costs

No one likes to push paper around, but if your investment business is to be successful, you must have control of the finances. You can do this by setting up a separate checkbook and credit card for all expense payments. It's easy to go back to these statements and develop spending reports, then compare the expenses against what you budgeted when you made your renovation cost estimates in Chapter 12, "Estimating Fix-Up Costs." Having a tight rein on the spending is especially important if you are doing the job yourself or acting as a general contractor. Every dollar you spend beyond your plan is one less dollar of potential profit.

Computerize Your Accounting

This type of accounting is very straightforward but takes time to set up. If you have invested in a computer and personal finance software as we suggested in Chapter 6, "Finding the Money," you already have the tools to organize and track this information.

The examples given here used Quicken Home & Business 2007, but any version of personal finance software is capable of providing the information you need, and all such programs work on the same principles. The programs allow you to set up multiple checking accounts and credit card accounts so that you can create custom categories to track expenses. You can easily configure these programs to track your spending and quickly produce reports showing where the money is going. They also allow you to create a budget representing your estimated job costs that you can compare with your actual spending. If you run all your spending through the program, it can give you a real-time picture of how your actual cost compares to your plan.

Here is a simplified example of how to use Quicken to manage your project.

After Quicken is up and running, create a Checking Account and Credit Card Account to track your expenses. You can use existing accounts, but we suggest that you create dedicated accounts for your real estate investments. Use the program's Cash Flow Center to create a Spending Account for checking (we named it Checking–Construction), and then set up a Credit Card Account named Credit Card–Construction. Of course, the real accounts that the computer is tracking must first be created at a financial institution.

Each transaction that is entered in the checking or credit account is tagged with a category that allows the software to arrange the transactions into meaningful reports. You can arrange and name categories any way you want, but we think that creating a master category like House Remodeling and then creating subcategories like Plumbing, Carpentry, and Bathroom makes logical sense. This way you have all your property renovation data under a single topic. The program can report on the total category or any subcategory.

To cut a check for floor refinishing (Figure 15.2), you would make out the check to the contractor and then in the category line choose the corresponding category from the drop-down menu. If you have used Fast Floor Service before, the program enters the address automatically; if not, type it in the address area and it will be stored for future use.

Figure 15.2

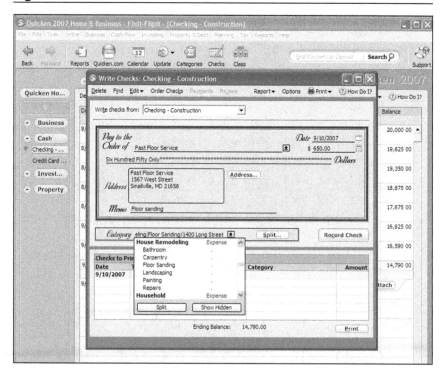

Eventually you will have more than one project, so you can use what Quicken calls "classes" to tag the expenses associated with specific projects. For example, if your first project was at 208 Maple Avenue and your current project is at 1400 Long Street, you would create a class for 208 Maple and a class for 1400 Long. Figure 15.3 shows a report of only the expenses for 1400 Long Street, even though there are many other expenses for 208 Maple in the system. By asking the program to create an expense report showing only those expenses in the 1400 Long class, you can zero in on a specific project. Of course, you could also create a report that shows only the Carpentry costs for 1400 Long.

The program also provides budgeting functions so that you can create a budget for a specific project and then create reports comparing the budget amounts to the actual money spent. Figure 15.4 shows a budget report giving the planned expenses (budget) for the 1400 Long project and the funds actually spent from the first of the year through the

Figure 15.3

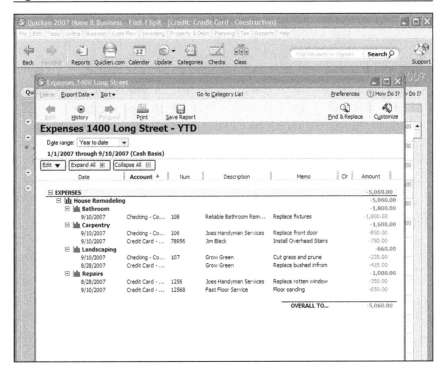

Figure 15.4

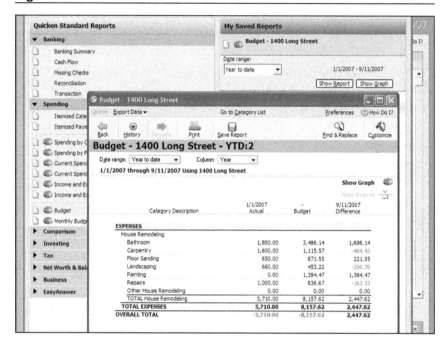

middle of September. This does not have to be limited to remodeling and renovation costs; you could also include closing, interest, and tax costs in this report. You just have to create a category for each type of expense you want to track; then with a keystroke you can see if everything is going according to plan.

Don't forget that "garbage in equals garbage out." If you don't take the time to enter the data, the computer can't generate meaningful answers. Quicken can lend a hand here, since it can download transactions from your bank and credit card provider and enter the transactions in the correct categories automatically. You can take this one step further and have Quicken print your checks or pay the bills online. These functions take a bit of time to set up, but they are well worth the effort.

Depending on your strategy, you may or may not be living in the house you are working on. If you are, the expenses will not be considered tax-deductible and you will not report them on your tax return. On the other hand, if you are not living in the property, then all expenses associated with purchasing, maintaining, improving, and selling the property are considered business expenses and are subtracted from any gain you make on the sale. Quicken can assign a tax classification to each expense or income category and prepare a report that is very helpful come income tax time. You can also import data from Quicken directly into Turbo Tax, one of the most popular income tax preparation software programs.

Checklist for Managing a Home Rehab

If you are willing to admit you're fallible, you'll agree that it's more than handy to have a reference for all the details involved in rehabbing a house, especially if you're managing the project. Even if you've hired a general contractor to make things happen, you should have a handle on the project and know how the work is progressing. The checklist we use is nothing more than a laundry list of the work required to bring a house to market. However you're involved in the work, adapt the checklist to your needs. Whether you use paper and a clipboard, a laptop, or a personal digital assistant, use the checklist in Figure 15.5 or make your own as a reference.

Figure 15.5 Checklist for Managing a Home Rehab

	WORK DESCRIPTION	COMPLETED
Exterior Siding		
Condition		
Other issues		
Foundation		
Support columns or piers		
Exterior Plumbing		
Spigot(s)		
Water meter		

	WORK DESCRIPTION	**COMPLETED**

Electrical Service

Meter   _____

Wires and cables   _____

Crawl Space

Condition of support posts, bolts   _____

Other issues   _____

Deck or Patio

Condition of material and railings   _____

Other issues   _____

Roof and Chimney

Flashing   _____

Gutters, downspouts, diverters   _____

Other issues   _____

Sidewalk and Driveway

Condition of surface, grading,
    low areas   _____

Other issues   _____

Doors and Storm Doors

Condition   _____

Lock   _____

Storm screen and glass panel   _____

Door threshold   _____

Other issues   _____

Windows and Storms

Condition   _____

Glass   _____

	WORK DESCRIPTION	**COMPLETED**
Caulking	_____	_____
Storm screen and glass panel	_____	_____
Other issues	_____	_____

Heating/Cooling Unit

Condition	_____	_____
Other issues	_____	_____

Garage, Outbuildings

Siding	_____	_____
Foundation and grading	_____	_____
Doors and windows	_____	_____
Roof, gutters, downspouts	_____	_____
Interior floor and walls	_____	_____
Electric power	_____	_____
Other issues	_____	_____

Landscaping and Trees

Lawn	_____	_____
Garden beds	_____	_____
Trees and shrubbery	_____	_____
Other issues	_____	_____

Living/Dining Room

Walls and ceiling	_____	_____
Doors	_____	_____
Windows	_____	_____
Floor	_____	_____
Fireplace	_____	_____
Built-ins	_____	_____

	WORK DESCRIPTION	COMPLETED
Electric outlets		
Lighting		
HVAC		
Other issues		

Kitchen

Walls and ceiling		
Doors		
Windows		
Floor		
Appliances: stove, oven, range, vent, refrigerator, disposal, dishwasher		
Sink and faucet		
Cabinets and countertops		
Electrical system		
GFCI outlets: adequate number and placement		
Lighting		
HVAC		
Other issues		

Electrical Service Panel

Bathroom 1

Walls and ceiling		
Doors		
Windows		
Floor		
Toilet		
Sink, faucet, cabinet		
Storage		

	WORK DESCRIPTION	COMPLETED
Accessories		
GFCI outlets: adequate number and placement		
Lighting		
HVAC		
Other issues		

Bathroom 2

Walls and ceiling		
Doors		
Windows		
Floor		
Toilet		
Sink, faucet, cabinet		
Storage		
Accessories		
GFCI outlets: adequate number and placement		
Lighting		
HVAC		
Other issues		

Bedroom 1

Walls and ceiling		
Doors		
Windows		
Floor		
Closet		
Electrical		
Lighting		

	WORK DESCRIPTION	COMPLETED
HVAC	_____	
Other issues	_____	
Bedroom 2		
Walls and ceiling	_____	
Doors	_____	
Windows	_____	
Floor	_____	
Closet	_____	
Electrical	_____	
Lighting	_____	
HVAC	_____	
Other issues	_____	
Bedroom 3		
Walls and ceiling	_____	
Doors	_____	
Windows	_____	
Floor	_____	
Closet	_____	
Electrical	_____	
Lighting	_____	
HVAC	_____	
Other issues	_____	
Family Room		
Walls and ceiling	_____	
Doors	_____	
Windows	_____	
Floor	_____	

	WORK DESCRIPTION	COMPLETED
Fireplace		
Built-ins		
Electrical		
Lighting		
HVAC		
Other issues		

Halls and Closets

Walls and ceiling		
Doors		
Windows		
Floor		
Stairs		
Smoke/CO detectors		
Other issues		

Attic

Finished, unfinished		
Rafters		
Ventilation		
Insulation		
Stairs and access		
Other issues		

Basement

Unfinished or partially finished		
Humidity, odors, water seepage		
Walls and ceiling		
Doors		
Windows		

	WORK DESCRIPTION	COMPLETED
Floor		
Lighting and electrical		
Plumbing pipes, water meter		
Stairs: balusters on steps, handrail on wall		
Other		
Laundry and appliances		
Dryer: secure hose connection; vent to outside, grounded		
Washer: braided stainless steel pressurized washer hoses, grounded		
Other issues		

Sump Pump and Floor Drain

Furnace or heat pump		
Secure ductwork, clean filter		
Other issues		

Hot-Water Heater

Gas or electric, adequate capacity		
Other issues		

Punch List

A punch list is a contractor's to-do list of everything that has not been completed and anything that requires fixing or replacement. As a property owner, you should keep a close eye on the progress of the work and keep your own punch list of things needing repair or correction. Use the list so that when you communicate regularly with the contractor, you can point out the items and look for others. Figure 15.6 is a sample contractor's punch list.

Figure 15.6 Punch List

Property owner _____

Property address _____

Contact information _____

General or subcontractor _____

Contact information _____

Punch List Items	**Date**	**Approved by**

Completed punch list items submitted by _____

Contractor _____

All items accepted as completed by _____

Owner _____

CHAPTER 16

SELLING FOR A PROFIT

The seller's responsibilities begin with getting the property ready for the market and end with handing over the keys to the house at the property settlement. By the time a rehabbed house is ready for the market, the work has been completed, and any broker should be pleased to show it. The first part of this chapter suggests additional steps to make the house as appealing as it can be. The rest of the chapter explains what's involved in the house-selling process, whether you're using a listing agent or selling "by owner."

On the Home Front

A recently renovated house without furniture can have a distinct advantage over a house full of furniture because the empty rooms make the property look more spacious. Buyers can imagine their furniture more easily when there's fresh paint on the walls, a clean floor, and none of those everyday things like toys and newspapers that give a house a lived-in look. Inside, you need to make the rooms look attractive and uncluttered so that the buyer is excited and wants to make the house his or her own. See the section "Secrets from House Stagers."

Before you post the "For Sale" sign in the yard and allow the house to be shown to anyone, take time for a final push to ensure that the house is clean and inviting. The goal is to create maximum curb appeal so that the first impression a buyer has when he or she pulls up in front of the house is positive.

Curb Appeal

A 2007 RealEstate.com survey of 500 sellers and 100 real estate agents across the country found that enhancing a lawn or landscape was the top priority in getting a house ready to sell. The respondents say that half of their clients' buying decisions are based on curb appeal. The real estate agents we know tell us the same thing: the initial impression that prospective buyers form when they first see a property is very important. They say it is difficult to get buyers to even get out of the car if they don't like what they see. So what makes a property have good curb appeal? That's not an easy question to answer because each buyer has individual tastes and expectations, but we can tell you that anything that hints of neglect is a turnoff.

The buyers' first impression is an overall wide-screen view of the property, so if it is favorable, they will probably want to take a closer look. Here are some low- or no-cost chores that can make a positive first impression on a prospective buyer. Time and money spent improving the curb appeal will provide some of the highest returns of any improvement you can make.

Squeaky-Clean and Inviting

These tidying-up chores and last-minute additions go a long way toward showing the house in its best light and indicating a pride of ownership that influences a prospective buyer. Remember, the house may have been a construction site for a while; you may be used to walking past piles of rubble, but the buyer is not.

Landscaping
During the period that the house is on the market and under contract, keep the lawn and garden trimmed and manicured. Make sure that the lawn is mowed regularly, the garden beds are edged, and the trees and shrubbery are trimmed.

Front Door
To make the front entrance inviting, lay down a new doormat and hang a wreath on the door. If weather permits, add a container of colorful flowers next to the door or on the porch, and keep them watered.

Garbage
Be vigilant about removing all garbage, debris, and scrap materials. Haul away or have removed anything that's old and unusable. Double-check that no construction debris has been left lying around. Rake the ground around the building to gather up paint chips and any old materials.

Light Fixtures
Go through the house and put new lightbulbs in the fixtures. If a room does not have a ceiling fixture, put a floor lamp in the room so that anyone touring the house at night will be able to see it. Put the lamp near the door so that if the house is shown in the evening, the broker can turn on the light easily. Change any lightbulbs in exterior lights, especially the lights at the front and back doors and garage.

Floors
Throughout the house, wash all floors and clean and vacuum the carpeting. Remove floor heating registers and vacuum inside them. Protect the clean floors at the front and back doors with a clean drop cloth or rug.

Closets
Remove hangers and clean out the shelves and floor of all closets. Check that the closet lights work.

Windows
Wash all the windows, including patio sliding doors.

Kitchen
Thoroughly clean all appliances, countertops, and kitchen cabinets, inside and out. If needed, add new shelf paper to line cabinet shelves.

Bathroom

Thoroughly clean all the fixtures, including the toilet, bathtub, and vanity cabinet. If you haven't already done so, make sure the tile grout is clean. Remove any mineral deposits on the showerhead.

Laundry Room

Thoroughly clean the washer and dryer, and remove any debris that was left in the area.

Attic, Basement, and Garage

If you have not painted the basement, use a shop vacuum to remove dust, dirt, and spiderwebs in the rafters and on the walls and floor. Remove any debris or materials that were left by the previous owner. Straighten and organize storm windows and other stored items that remain with the house. Check that the light fixtures are in working order.

If You Are Living in the House

Declutter everywhere, removing stacks of newspapers and magazines and stuff inside closets and cabinets. Use three boxes for the stuff you remove: one box to toss, sell, or donate; another to keep; and one for stuff in limbo that you can't decide about.

Don't have a television in the living room. It adds to the clutter and tips buyers off that the house is so small that this is the only place for the TV. Remove the coffeemaker, can opener, and other appliances in the kitchen to free up countertop space. Remove a third of the furnishings in every room to make the house appear more spacious. Organize and clean bookcases and shelves throughout the house.

Secrets from House Stagers

A stager is a designer or someone with design experience who helps a homeowner market his or her house to its full potential. Stagers usually work with sellers in a sluggish market to help them sell their house. Sometimes developers of new homes hire a stager for customers to get them out of their old home and into their new one. The stager surveys the property and makes specific recommendations. Frequently the listing real estate broker brings in a stager to suggest changes that edit out the extraneous items that have meaning for the owners but do nothing to make the house appealing to a buyer. To put it bluntly, they usually recommend getting rid of most of the precious personal stuff, cumbersome collections, and trinkets that fill up many homes. They pare down closets so that they look spacious, not crammed full. And they often suggest that sellers rent a storage unit to store their excess furnishings while the house is on the market.

They start with the obvious: clean the house thoroughly, make it smell fresh, and get rid of stuff to make the house appear larger. Stagers know that time-stretched buyers want a turnkey house, one that's ready to move into and doesn't require remodeling. Stagers routinely suggest painting the walls and ceilings and replacing old carpeting. They often suggest replacing clashing or outdated wallpaper with a basic paint job. Once the decorating is completed, they rearrange the pared-down furnishings and sometimes bring in their own accessories to add props to the house.

On the Sales Front

The process involved in selling the house is the same as the process when you are a buyer; however, your perspective as the seller is different. If you use a real estate broker to list the property, the listing agent takes on the responsibility of advertising, showing the house, and representing your interests when a buyer makes an offer to purchase the house. If you sell the property "by owner," those responsibilities fall on you. Of course, selling a house yourself puts more money in your pocket because you don't have to pay a commission.

As you get the house ready to sell, it's important that you have a handle on the local real estate market. In less than a year, the market can move from a seller's market to a buyer's market, with more properties for sale than there are buyers. It's harder to underprice a property in a seller's market than it is to overprice a property in a buyer's market. Just because the house down the street sold for X dollars does not mean that your property will sell for the same price if the market has changed.

Today, in September 2007, we have definitely moved from a seller's to a buyer's market so, except in some very select markets, buyers are no longer bidding against one another for a particular property. Instead, home sellers are competing with their neighbors to sell their property.

Discover Potential Problems Before the Sale

The most important thing to remember is that the same tactics that you as the buyer used to get a good deal can be used against you as the seller. Any problem with the property that a home inspector may turn up can cost you more to negotiate during the sale than it would to fix beforehand.

Hiring a home inspector to do a presale inspection is money well spent. Most home inspectors will charge considerably less for a presale inspection if you do not require an extensive report. There's more about hiring a home inspector in Chapter 11, "Buying the Property."

A presale inspection will help you identify any problems that you have overlooked that could prevent or delay the sale of the house. There's nothing worse than getting a nice offer, accepting it, and then having a home inspection turn up a serious termite problem. You should take care of any major problem before you place the property on the market but there may be some things you overlooked or thought were minor that the home inspector may not agree with. It is better to take care of these conditions before the house is on the market.

If any problems are detected, discuss them with the inspector, an attorney, or your real estate broker. Most state real estate sales laws make it your responsibility as the seller to disclose information about defects in the property that could influence someone's decision to buy the house. These include structural defects and health risks such as lead, asbestos, radon, formaldehyde, and carbon monoxide.

Listing with a Real Estate Broker

A listing agreement is a written contract that spells out the legal relationship between a seller and a real estate brokerage firm. It states that the property owner gives the real estate company a specified amount of time to sell the property and receive a commission (a percentage of the sales price). Some sellers retain the right to sell the property themselves (and not pay a commission), but this doesn't hold much appeal for a real estate company that is going to spend time and money advertising and showing the property.

A listing agreement should include the following items:

- The name and location of the property and the owner
- The listing real estate broker and company
- Sales price
- Commission
- Type of listing
- Length of contract (expiration date)
- Signatures
- Termination clause if either party wants to cancel the contract
- Items included in the sale of the property, e.g., appliances, window treatments, carpeting
- Offers and how and when they are presented
- Deposit of earnest money
- Broker responsibilities

When a seller signs a listing agreement with a broker, the two parties are entering into a partnership with one goal in mind: finding a buyer for the property and closing the deal. The job of the property owner is to hand over the keys to a house that is clean and appealing and then get out of the way and let the professionals show the house to prospective buyers. The listing broker submits the listing to the listing service he or she subscribes to, which then gives the information to a network of real estate brokers. One day a week on a regular basis, there is an open house for real estate agents to tour recently listed properties. These agents have client rosters of buyers looking for specific types of houses in specific neighborhoods, so there is often a flurry of showings after the agents see a new listing and make appointments with prospective clients.

For Sale by Owner (FSBO)

We think there are far more disadvantages than advantages to selling by owner. An owner-seller can't compete with the hundreds of brokers with qualified buyers who are interested in buying a house—possibly the one you have for sale. Maybe if after rehabbing and selling several investment properties, you want to tackle the job, it's worth considering. But for the first-time investor, definitely plan to pay a broker to list and sell your property.

You're more likely to be successful at selling an investment property yourself if the market is very active, with more buyers than sellers. You also must have a flexible schedule that allows you to show the property at any time. You must be available to meet prospective buyers at their convenience, which can be day or night or on weekends.

A sales background is a plus for an owner-seller, who will need to meet and greet strangers, listen to their comments, and respond to negative comments about the house with positives. It helps to have a knowledge of financing and connections with lenders if you're acting as your own agent, especially if your property is being marketed to first-time home buyers. They need someone to hold their hands through all the phases of qualifying for a loan and then processing the application and completing the forms. That sales expertise also comes into play when the deal is finalized and loose ends need to be tied up and contracts signed. If you are thinking about selling by owner, definitely plan to hire a real estate lawyer to represent you so that you leave nothing to chance.

Evaluating an Offer to Purchase

There are three basic things to consider when a broker presents you, the seller, with an offer: the price, the financial terms, and the closing date. If there is more than one offer, the listing broker should present them all at the same time for comparison. Because investment property is ready for occupancy, closing sooner rather than later is the priority. The best offer may not always be the one with the highest price. Take into consideration how qualified the buyer is. A fast closing date will save you money and get you your cash more quickly. Look at the sale in total, not just the price.

Making a Counteroffer

Unless you are selling the property yourself, the actual negotiating over the price and terms of the contract is the job of the real estate broker; that's what you're paying him or her for. If the offer does not meet your expectations, talk it over with the broker and instruct him or her to make a counteroffer.

Use the seller's checklist in Figure 16.1 to guide you through the responsibilities and process of selling your house.

Figure 16.1 Seller's Checklist

Before you sign a contract to list your property for sale, take the time to make the property as desirable and market-ready as you can. Use this checklist to guide you through the sales process.

TASKS	DATE	NOTES
Order a presale inspection of the property		
Review the terms of the listing contract		
Complete all improvement projects		
Complete all cleaning tasks		
Remove all garbage, debris, and materials		
Check that home insurance coverage includes the house being on the market		
Order an extra set of keys for the broker		
Consult with utility companies about changing names on service records		
Schedule a final walk-through		
Review final settlement statement		
Arrange to make loan payoff with lender		
Stop service on all utilities		
Discontinue insurance		
Get address of settlement location		
Make loan payoff to lender		

Tax Advantage After the Sale

One of the big advantages of owning real estate is how favorably it is treated by the tax code. We have been able to use this to our advantage over the 30 years or so that we have been working on houses. During this time, the tax laws have changed, and no doubt they are going to change in the future, but the favorable treatment of homeownership has survived.

Owner-Occupied

If you live in a house that you own and then sell it, the first $250,000 for an individual or $500,000 for a couple is tax-free. The current law allows you to do this every two years. Just how long you have to live in the house is open to some question, but when we lived in a house, it usually took us a few years to completely renovate it and get it back on the market. Our strategy is to live in the house that has the greatest potential for profit.

Non-Owner-Occupied

If you don't live in the property but you hold it for more than a year while you are working on it, the gain on the sale may qualify as a capital gain. Capital gains are taxed at a 20 percent rate, which may be lower than your current tax rate. In either case, the profit from the sale will not be taxed at a higher rate than your overall tax-bracket rate. This will hold up unless you buy and sell so many properties that the IRS considers you a dealer, and then you must pay straight tax.

Rental Property

Rental property can be traded for like property, and no tax on the transaction will be due. This has tax advantages, but so far we haven't used the strategy. There are plenty of books on the subject and plenty of tax advisors out there on how to report a 1031 type transaction. The IRS publishes a bulletin Like-Kind Exchanges - Real Estate Tax Tips found on their Web site www.irs.gov.

Tax Savings Are Not Enough

The most important thing to remember about taxes is that property must sell for a profit for you to save on taxes. Buying property and selling it for a loss may be a great tax write-off, but it makes for a poor business plan. The real estate investments you make must stand on their own merits. If a positive cash flow does not result from the deal, then it's not worth doing. The tax breaks that are available increase the amount of the profit you get to keep, but tax breaks alone don't generate profits.

CHAPTER 17

RENTING AS A FALLBACK STRATEGY

R enting real estate is a good business in itself. Purchasing a single-family property, fixing it up, and then renting it out to cover the holding costs has been a long-term strategy of many investors. But the primary focus of this book is on renovating property for resale. We use rental as a fallback to cover the expense of holding property through a market swing. A rental situation that covers most, if not all, of the holding costs during that time has allowed us to weather several sluggish markets.

Rents have not kept up with the large runup in house prices in most markets, so it's difficult to produce a large positive cash flow from renting a single-family house. (Of course, the exception is in vacation areas, where daily, weekly, or monthly rentals produce a good return on investment. But it's often seasonal, not year-round, rental income.) However, we have found that the rent covered most of the cost of holding the property, including mortgage service, taxes, and maintenance.

Until the meltdown of the real estate market in 2007, monthly mortgage payments were in many cases actually less than the cost of renting a single-family house or apartment of the same size. Needless to say, the rental market suffered a bit. Now, with the rising cost of financing and tougher underwriting standards, some buyers have been priced out of the market. The result is that rents are on the rise and occupancy rates are falling as potential buyers turn to rental units for housing. So for an investor with a property ready for market, renting the property may be a better decision than trying to sell it in a buyer's market.

In Chapter 7, we suggest that you consider the ability to rent the property in your purchasing evaluation, so the first requirement for a rental fallback strategy is to invest in property that can be rented. However, renting the property ties up your working capital. This may not be a problem, but if you are just starting, the money you need to purchase another property will be tied up in your current project.

If you do consider renting, here are some ideas that you can use to find tenants, screen them, and then manage the property.

Finding Tenants

Many people who were priced out of the buying market will find that they have more rental properties to choose from because many sellers who don't find a buyer will choose to rent their property. The problem of finding a buyer will probably be made worse because a large percentage of investors who bought second homes and other single-family properties may be forced to sell as adjustable-rate mortgages begin to reset. This is something to think about before you sign up for some of the more exotic loan products.

The Internet has become a primary source for rental listings, so don't overlook this medium. Locally, print flyers and circulate them around the neighborhood. Post them on bulletin boards in grocery stores, the post office, and anywhere else that allows posting of local ads. If you are allowed to, don't forget to put a "For Rent" sign in front of the property. Read the advertisements of your competitors to see if they are offering incentives. If your advertisement does not produce results, consider sweetening your offer and holding an open house.

Screening Tenants

The biggest mistake we have made in renting our properties has been not checking the tenants carefully. We would collect the information, but then we'd check out only a few references. Don't make this mistake. Check out everything; go down the application line by line and call everyone. It doesn't take long, and the information will give you a good picture of the reliability of the applicant. See Figure 17.1 for an example of a tenant application form.

Figure 17.1 Tenant Application

Tenant Name	_____
Employer Name	_____
Monthly Income	_____
Credit and Bank Information	_____
Bank	_____
Checking	_____
Savings	_____
Credit Cards	_____
Credit Report Authorization	_____
Auto Information	_____
Driver's License	_____
License Plate Number	_____
Rental History (list three)	_____
	_____
	_____
Personal References (list three)	_____
	_____
	_____

It does not matter whether you like your tenants; it does matter that they pay the rent on time, so get an authorization from them to run a credit check and do it. There are Web sites that specialize in running credit checks for landlords. Use Google to do a search, or use the one at www.Mrlandlord.com.

Probably the least important item on the application is the personal references. The applicant will not list a poor reference, and most people avoid bad-mouthing anyone. This is especially true for family members, but check them out anyway; this may be the deciding factor between two strong applicants.

Remember that state and federal laws prohibit you from discriminating against a tenant based on race, sex, age, gender, family status or size, nationality, or disability. You must have a good business reason, such as poor credit or a bad reference, to reject a tenant. Keep good records, and retain all the applications for your records. You should choose the applicant with the best credit and references, so document each tenant's application to establish a paper trail.

Lease

A lease is a legal contract between you, as the landlord, and the tenant that spells out the relationship in detail. Since tenant-landlord relations have not always been cordial, there has been a lot of litigation over leases; consequently, many states have passed laws requiring certain clauses to be included in the lease. There is no standard form, although you may find what purports to be one at an office supplier. The best way to get a lease that is legal in your state is to go to a legal forms Web site like www.FindLegalForms.com and download a copy that is approved for your state.

Fill out the lease form carefully and have your tenants look it over carefully. They may want to consult their lawyer, which is a common practice. Just about every point on the lease is negotiable. If the tenant returns the lease with modifications, look it over carefully; remember that it's your property and you set the rules.

The main thing we have learned in dealing with tenants is that the lease is only as good as the integrity of the parties signing the document. If tenants violate the terms of the lease, such as by not paying the rent, notify them in writing immediately or as soon as you become aware of the problem. If the tenants do not correct the problem, take action. When you are renting only a single unit, this can be a big problem, since it's you that has to deal with the tenant and not "the property manager."

Rent

The local market sets the rents, but rentals are not all created equal. A bit of research will show that there is a wide variance in the rent that people will pay for the same size units. It's not rocket science to figure out that the better the location and the nicer the house, the more rent it can command. However, there is a point of diminishing returns beyond which the state of the property, no matter how nice, will not command more rent; it will just make it easier to rent.

So when you are faced with a buyer's market, it may be a better strategy to fix up the property so that it can be rented, but hold off on major renovations until the market improves. A clean house with a fresh coat of paint and all the appliances working may produce rent close to what a fully renovated unit would produce, with a lot less investment on your part. A little research can bear this out. Remember, a rental unit suffers from wear and tear, no matter how good the tenant is.

Cash Flow

Running a rental property is an ongoing enterprise, so the measure of success is whether the property can be rented for more that the expenses of holding and maintaining it. If the rent exceeds the expenses, the property is said to produce a positive cash flow; if the expenses exceed the rent, you must make up the difference and you have a negative cash flow.

Accounting

Accounting for a rental property is a bit different from accounting for a renovation project that produces no income to report to the IRS until the property is sold. Rental property generates income in the form of rent, and that rent must be reported in the year it is earned. Expenses like interest, property taxes, depreciation, utilities, advertising, and repairs are deductible. You pay income tax on the difference between the rent income and the expenses. If you have a positive cash flow, you will owe taxes on this amount; if there is a negative cash flow, then the loss can be deducted from your other income.

The Tax code allows you to deduct a portion of the value of the property, but not the land each year on the Income Tax form. Since depreciation is a noncash expense you don't actually pay anyone for the depreciation cost so if the rent is more than the expenses you could have a positive cash flow but report a loss on your tax form because of the depreciation charge.

Your income or loss on your rental property must be reported on your income tax return, so you should keep good records of both rents paid in and expenses paid out. The easiest way to do this is to use the same personal financial software we discussed in Chapter 15. Open a separate checking account for rent deposits and then set up income categories for the rent and categories for the expenses. At income tax time, all you have to do is print out a report.

Quicken also allows you to tag each category with the corresponding income tax–related item on the 1040 federal individual tax form. This takes a bit of time to set up, but you can then export this information directly into TurboTax and that program will take care of the rest. It will also prepare your state and local taxes.

Tax Implications

One expense category that you should do a bit of planning for is depreciation which allows you to account for the wear and tear of the property. The tax code allows you to depreciate the house but not the land. Depreciation is allowed because theoretically an asset (such as a piece of machinery) eventually wears out and becomes worthless. Of course, unless you neglect the property, it will grow in value over time. So the law allows you to depreciate the property, but when you sell the property, you must use the depreciated value as your cost basis. This lower basis makes your potential profit larger, and you will have to pay taxes on this amount. Of course, if you lose money there is no profit and therefore no tax.

The depreciation of an asset that appreciates is a way of deferring taxes. The IRS has free publications on business expenses and depreciation at www.irs.gov.

In the last 5 chapters there are many worksheets that you can copy directly out of the book and reproduce yourself. These and other calculators are also included on the CD-Rom contained in the companion workbook.

CHAPTER 18

TIMELINE FOR A FAST FIX IT AND FLIP IT (UNDER 60 DAYS)

This timeline is for making various cosmetic improvements to a three-bedroom ranch located in a good neighborhood. It had been rental property and showed signs of neglect by both the renters and the landlord. While the house was standard issue, we saw its potential because of its location and the attractive stone fireplace in the living room. The house was on a quarter-acre lot with dense, overgrown bushes and shrubbery and a foot-high lawn. The exterior siding and windows were vinyl-clad and in good condition, but a deck off the back of the house had been covered with outdoor carpeting that had rotted the decking.

Inside, the rooms were all painted yellow. The living room, hall, and three bedrooms were all carpeted in worn, rust-colored carpeting, and there was a patch of chipped and broken ceramic tile at the entry. The carpeting held the smells of pets that had previously lived in the house, making it a real turnoff to potential buyers. The kitchen and dining area had a wild-patterned green and yellow vinyl floor. The wooden cabinets and laminate countertop were in acceptable condition. The bathroom had wall tile with a bathtub and toilet in acceptable condition. At least half of the electric switches and receptacles had to be replaced because they were caked with layers of paint, and those in the kitchen and bathroom would not meet the building codes.

Measure-and-Make-Notes Visit

Before closing on the property and taking possession, we had an afternoon to assess the property. During this measure-and-make-notes visit, we took room measurements and determined the specific improvements and upgrades that we needed to make.

After the visit, we made initial calls to price and order a Dumpster. We had delivery of the Dumpster scheduled for our first week in the house so that we could fill it with all the things we tore out. This included the carpeting, padding, flooring, and other materials; debris left in the yard; and piles of tree and shrubbery branches that we had left over after pruning and grooming.

In the weeks before taking possession, we made several shopping trips to home centers, flooring outlets, and hardware stores to explore styles, colors, and prices of carpeting, vinyl flooring, lighting fixtures, kitchen appliances, and replacements for the bathroom.

We both planned to work on the house full-time along with hiring two specialty contractors: one to rebuild the deck and another to repair termite damage to the south wall of the house. Before closing on the property, we made initial calls to contractors to get estimates and to schedule the work for a time when we were there working on the house. We had both contractors come with us on the walk-through, and we discussed what had to be done to repair the wall and the deck. The carpenter who would be repairing the termite damage to the sill and foundation decided that all the work could be done from the outside of the house. Only the lower portion of the wall was affected, so the siding could be removed, the damaged portion of the wall studs and sill repaired, and the siding replaced. The deck builder was also going to work outside the house, so our work inside the house wouldn't be affected by either of them.

We ordered cleaning supplies and off-white latex paint in five-gallon containers for the walls and ceiling (flat) and the trim (semigloss). We organized the tools and equipment we thought we would need so that we would be ready as soon as we took possession. This included a garbage can, plastic garbage bags, a hand toolbox, a ladder, a shop vacuum, demolition tools, garden hose, a lawn mower and pruning tools, a work light, power tools, heavy-duty extension cords, and workhorses. We planned to set up two staging areas: one with a source of water for paint cleanup and another for storing tools and materials.

Week 1

The goal for the first week was to fill the Dumpster and get rid of unwanted materials and appliances. The longer we kept the Dumpster, the more it would cost, so we planned to fill it as quickly as possible with yard waste after extensive pruning and cutting back of the overgrown landscape. Then we loaded it with trash and debris that had been left on the property. The projects inside and out didn't affect each other, and we could revise our work plan based on the weather.

Day 1

- Checked all doors and windows for operation or repair work and noted the results on the checklist.
- Changed the exterior door locks.
- Removed the bathroom vanity and faucet, medicine cabinet, light fixture, and floor and ceiling registers.
- Disconnected the refrigerator and range and moved them to the Dumpster.
- Took down and threw out all draperies, shades, and hardware and the shower curtain and rod.
- Removed all base shoe molding around the rooms for a better-fitting new-carpet installation; tossed molding (not worth saving) into the Dumpster.
- Tore up and removed all wall-to-wall carpeting and padding in the living room, hall, and three bedrooms, including the old carpeting tacks and some tacks left in the floor from previous installations.
- Chipped out and removed a three- by five-foot ceramic tile pad at the entry to the living room.

Day 2

- Removed vinyl flooring and adhesive in the kitchen and laundry.
- Vacuumed all windows and floors.
- Did "first-cut" lawn mowing and raked up clippings.
- Made a second pass with the mower and raked up clippings.
- Began pruning the row of shrubbery lining the sides of the property.

Day 3

- Continued pruning the shrubbery lining the sides of the property.
- Removed debris left in the backyard and shed (rotten landscape timbers, broken lawn furniture, car tires, old grill, and rusty yard tools and mower).
- Pruned four trees.
- Checked all electric switches and receptacles to see whether they worked or needed to be replaced; removed all switch plate covers and marked their location on the back side; made count for new plate covers and replacement devices needed.

Day 4

- Pruned all the evergreens in front of the house.
- Pruned all the shrubbery across the rear of the property.
- Looked for bare spots in the lawn and weeded, seeded, and watered.
- Edged all garden beds.

Day 5

- Throughout the house, removed window hardware and interior door lock sets, washed all surfaces, and let them dry.
- Throughout the house, removed all ceiling light fixtures.
- Installed new switches and outlets where needed, then covered all switches and receptacles with masking tape to protect them from paint.

Week 2

This week's goal was to get the interior of the house ready to paint. Patching and priming the interior was a major job because many of the walls required at least two applications of wallboard compound. The same was true for the woodwork and trim. Because the walls and woodwork were painted yellow, everything needed a prime coat before painting. Removing the black mastic that held some cork tiles to the dining room wall presented the biggest challenge.

Day 6

- Laid down drop cloths on all floors.
- Applied wide masking tape along the fireplace walls to protect them from paint.
- Prepared walls and ceiling in the living room, hall, and three bedrooms by removing nails; filling holes, cracks, and nail pops with a first application of wallboard compound; and letting it dry.
- Prepared woodwork and trim around windows and doors in the living room, hall, and three bedrooms by filling in holes and cracks with interior spackling compound and letting it dry.

Day 7

- In the living room, hall, and three bedrooms, sanded the first applications of the compounds filling the wallboard and woodwork, then made a second application to fill in voids and let it dry.
- In kitchen-dining area, laid down drop cloths on countertops.
- Removed the cork tiles on the dining-area wall and used a heat gun on the black mastic adhesive.
- Made repairs to holes and a structural crack uncovered after removal of the cork wall.
- Applied stain killer to the black spots left by the mastic adhesive from the cork wall.

Day 8

- Sanded repairs to what had been the cork wall and applied a skim coat of drywall compound.
- In the living room, hall, and three bedrooms, sanded the second applications of compounds filling the wallboard and woodwork.
- Prepared the walls and ceiling in the kitchen-dining area by removing nails; filling holes, cracks, and nail pops with a first application of wallboard compound; and letting it dry.
- Prepared the woodwork and trim around windows and doors in the kitchen-dining area by filling in holes and cracks with interior spackling compound and letting it dry.
- Applied wide masking tape around cabinets to protect them from primer and paint.

Day 9

- Sanded the skim coat of drywall compound on what had been the cork wall and made a second application of compound.
- In the kitchen-dining area, sanded the first applications of the compounds to the walls, ceilings, and woodwork, then made a second application to fill in voids and let it dry.
- Removed all switch and receptacle covers in the kitchen and replaced the outlets with GFCIs and new switches.
- Wrapped masking tape around the outlets and switches to protect them from paint.

Day 10

- Sanded the cork wall skim coat and all walls, ceilings, and woodwork in the kitchen-dining area.
- Vacuumed all walls, ceilings, woodwork, and floors.
- Washed the exterior of the kitchen cabinets.
- Shook out drop cloths and put them back in place.
- Applied latex PVA primer to the walls and ceilings in the living room, hall, three bedrooms, and kitchen-dining area.

Week 3

The goals for this week were getting a final coat of paint on all the rooms and the woodwork around doors and windows, including the closet and room doors, and beginning work in the bathroom.

Day 11

- Applied the first coat of paint to the ceilings and walls in the living room, hall, and three bedrooms.

Day 12

- Applied the final coat of paint to the ceilings and walls in the kitchen-dining area.
- Applied the first coat of paint to the woodwork and trim in the living room, hall, and three bedrooms.

Day 13

- Applied the second coat of paint to the woodwork and trim in the living room, hall, and three bedrooms.

Day 14

- Applied the first coat of paint to the woodwork and trim in the kitchen-dining area.
- Prepared the bathroom by washing the ceiling, painted and tiled walls, window trim, and door.
- Made the first application of epoxy repair system to rebuild the rotten windowsill in the tub surround.

Day 15

- Applied the second coat of paint to the woodwork and trim in the kitchen-dining area.
- Scrubbed the bathtub, tiles, grout, and faucet.

- Removed the indoor carpeting tiles on the bathroom floor.
- Sanded the epoxy and made the second application to the windowsill.

Week 4

This week's goals were to complete the bathroom and make repairs to the exterior doors.

Day 16

- Applied masking tape on the edge of the bathroom wall tiles to protect them from paint.
- Sanded the second application of epoxy to the windowsill and applied primer.
- Repaired the exterior trim around the patio door by scraping the wood trim, priming bare spots, filling in holes, and sanding; also cleaned out the track so that the panels would slide freely.
- Replaced the handle on the interior of the patio door.
- Removed the doorknob and knocker of the front door.
- Vacuumed and cleaned the entryway threshold.

Day 17

- Painted the walls and ceiling in the bathroom.
- Sanded the wood trim around the patio door and painted it.
- Used a heat gun to remove layers of paint from the front door.

Day 18

- Painted the window trim and door in the bathroom.
- Filled in holes and cracks in the front door.
- Washed walls and trim and filled in holes in the laundry area.

Day 19

- Installed a new vanity and faucet, shower curtain rod, medicine cabinet, and light fixture in the bathroom; replaced the toilet seat.
- Installed new ceiling and floor registers throughout the house.
- Washed the bathroom floor.
- Repaired the tracks on the bedroom closet doors.
- Installed smoke and CO detectors.
- Mowed the lawn.

Day 20

- Sanded the surface of the front door and applied primer.
- Washed the interior of the kitchen cabinets and lined them with shelf paper.
- Cleaned the dishwasher.
- Vacuumed the furnace and replaced the filter.
- Washed the utility area around the hot-water heater.

Week 5

At the beginning of the week, the goal was to finish up most of our work in preparation for the carpeting and flooring installation. Then the objectives were to complete cleaning the exterior and make final installations of light fixtures and window blinds and to install the kitchen floor before the refrigerator and range were delivered.

Day 21

- Painted the ceiling, walls, and trim in the laundry room.
- Painted the front door.
- Installed new lighting fixtures throughout the house.
- Installed a new house number plaque on the siding.

Day 22

- Washed the laundry room floor.
- Cleaned out the gutters and installed new splash blocks.
- Power-washed the siding.
- Repaired torn screens.
- Had carpeting installed in the living room, hall, and three bedrooms.
- Installed a new knocker on the front door.

Day 23

- Had vinyl flooring installed in the kitchen-dining area.
- Trimmed doors that were too tight on the new carpeting.
- Installed new hardware on the interior doors.
- Washed all windows inside and out.
- Painted the base shoe molding for the kitchen-dining area floors.
- Installed new window miniblinds.

Day 24

- Installed new base shoe molding in the kitchen-dining area and touched up paint as needed.
- Hooked up the new range and refrigerator.
- Installed a new vertical blind on the patio glider door.
- Mowed the lawn.
- Removed all painting equipment.

Day 25

- Removed all tools and materials.
- Invited the real estate listing broker to view the house.

CHAPTER 19

TIMELINE FOR A SPACE-EXPANDING MAKEOVER THAT INCREASED RESALE VALUE (SIX MONTHS)

This timeline features an expandable two-bedroom Cape Cod with an unfinished attic. The work involved improving and redecorating the first floor of the house, which included a living room, dining room, kitchen, bath, utility room, and two bedrooms. Then we built a dormer, creating two bedrooms, a hall, and a bathroom upstairs. The exterior of the house was given a coat of paint, making it appear totally new from the outside. We transformed the house from a two-bedroom, one-bath home to one with four bedrooms and two baths. The work took approximately five months to complete, and the house was put on the market in the sixth month.

The house was unusual in that it had been owned by a woman who was a hoarder. Every room was filled waist-high with furniture and piles of stuff. It was difficult to see the walls of the house, let alone the floors, because the rooms were overstuffed with furniture that was stacked with piles of newspapers, magazines, old clothing, and just about anything else under the sun.

Before taking possession, we ordered a Dumpster to be delivered and hired two helpers to sort through all the stuff that had been left there. We invited everyone we knew to come and take what they wanted. Goodwill picked up some of the furnishings, and some things were donated to charity, but most of the objects were destined to fill three Dumpsters.

We removed the refrigerator (which was filled with spoiled food), range, and flooring in the kitchen and the vanity, medicine cabinet, and flooring in the bathroom. Throughout the house, we removed draperies, window shades, and carpeting.

The land around the house was also laden with debris and miscellaneous car engines and parts. The lawn and shrubbery were overgrown, but there was salvageable low shrubbery framing the front door and the side entrance. The driveway was a patchwork of asphalt that needed repairs and resurfacing.

It took two weeks to completely empty the house and tame the yard. We were surprised to find that the walls and floors were actually in pretty fair shape. There was mildew in areas of the bathroom and kitchen, but the walls were sound and the oak floors were worn but could be restored by refinishing.

Because the attic was also filled to capacity, we had to wait until the second week to measure the space and assess the additional rooms that we planned to build. We knew that the house had been built for expansion because the heating ducts were installed but capped off. The stairs were wide and in the center of the house, so the layout of the second floor was easy to determine. At the top of the stairs, we designed a hall with the new bathroom over the first-floor bathroom and a bedroom on either side of it.

We painted the living room, dining room, and hall in a flat, off-white latex paint and used a satin finish on the woodwork and trim. We hung wallpaper in the two bedrooms downstairs and the kitchen and painted all the new rooms upstairs in the same off-white.

We did most of the work ourselves, occasionally hiring helpers when we needed them. We hired a roofing contractor to reroof the entire house, and we had a flooring retailer install the carpeting.

Month 1

The top priority for the first month was to remove the clutter and debris inside and around the property. Then the objective was to plan and design the layout of the attic expansion and apply for a building permit. While waiting for the permit, the goal was to work on cleaning and decorating the first floor. Here is a rough timeline of how the work progressed.

Weeks 1 and 2

- Checked all the doors and windows to see if they were operational; opened the windows to air out the house; changed the exterior door locks.
- Removed the contents of the house and yard, filling three Dumpsters.
- Took measurements of the attic.

Week 3

- Designed a floor plan for the dormer and attic expansion.
- Made an application for a building permit to expand the second floor.
- Measured the rooms to estimate and order painting and wallpaper supplies.
- Set up two staging areas: a wet workstation in the utility room with a washtub for cleaning out paintbrushes and rollers and storing paint, and a dry workstation in the living room to store tools, materials, and a radio.
- Brought in cleaning supplies, power tools, workhorses, garbage bags, a hand toolbox, a ladder, a shop vacuum, demolition tools, garden hose, a lawn mower, and pruning gear.
- Vacuumed all the windows and floors.
- Throughout the house, checked all electric switches and receptacles to see if they worked or needed to be replaced; made a count of new plate covers and replacement devices needed.
- Laid down drop cloths in all rooms on the first floor.
- Throughout the house, removed the window hardware, doorknobs, and lock sets and cleaned and polished them.
- Throughout the house, removed all ceiling light fixtures and replaced them with temporary light fixtures.
- Mowed the lawn.

Week 4

- Removed the wallpaper in two bedrooms and the dining room.
- Washed the walls in two bedrooms and the dining room to remove adhesive and washed the windows, doors, woodwork, and trim.
- Prepped the ceiling in two bedrooms by filling cracks and nail pops with a first application of wallboard compound and letting it dry.
- Prepped the windows, doors, woodwork, and baseboard trim in two bedrooms by filling in holes and cracks with interior spackling compound and letting it dry.
- Sanded the first applications of the compounds filling the ceiling, woodwork, and trim, then made a second application to fill in voids and let it dry.
- Sanded the second application of compounds on the bedroom ceilings, windows, doors, woodwork, and trim.
- Painted the ceilings in two bedrooms.
- Painted the doors, windows, woodwork, and trim in two bedrooms.
- Applied sizing to the walls of two bedrooms.
- Hung wallpaper in two bedrooms.
- Worked out final details of the second-floor addition with the Building Department.
- Mowed the lawn.

Month 2

The goal for this month was to clean and decorate most of the rooms on the first floor. Although the eat-in kitchen was small, it required considerable time because we painted the cabinets, which needed extensive preparation and sanding. We also made out the materials list for the second-floor addition.

Week 5

- Prepped the walls and ceilings in the living room, dining room, and hall by removing nails; filling holes, cracks, and nail pops with a first application of wallboard compound; and letting it dry.
- Prepped the doors, windows, woodwork, and trim in the living room, dining room, and hall by filling in holes and cracks with interior spackling compound and letting it dry.
- Sanded the first application of wallboard compound in the living room, dining room, and hall, then made a second application to fill in voids and let it dry.
- Sanded the first applications of spackling compound in the living room, dining room, and hall windows, woodwork, and trim, then made a second application to fill in voids and let it dry.
- Sanded the second applications of compounds on the ceilings, walls, woodwork, and trim in the living room, dining room, and hall.
- Removed all switch plate covers and marked their location on the back side.
- Installed replacement switches and GFCI receptacles and wrapped them with masking tape to protect them from paint.
- Painted the ceilings and walls in the living room, dining room, and hall.
- Mowed the lawn and trimmed the shrubbery.

Week 6

- Painted the doors, windows, woodwork, and trim in the living room, dining room, and hall.
- Reinstalled the door and window hardware in the living room, dining room, hall, and bedrooms.
- Removed all switch and receptacle covers in the kitchen and replaced the outlets with GFCIs and new switches.
- Removed the wallpaper in the kitchen.

- Washed the kitchen ceiling, walls, windows, doors, woodwork, and trim.
- Washed the kitchen cabinets inside and out.
- Repaired the ceiling in kitchen by removing nails; filling holes, cracks, and nail pops with a first application of wallboard compound; and letting it dry.
- Applied wallboard compound to large cracks in the kitchen wall that were discovered when the wallpaper was removed, and let it dry.
- Sanded the first application of wallboard compound on the kitchen ceiling, then applied a second coat and let it dry.
- Sanded the first application of wallboard compound to the cracks in kitchen wall, then applied a second coat of wallboard compound to the cracks in the kitchen wall with a coat of PVA primer.
- Sanded the second coat of wallboard compound on the kitchen ceiling.
- Painted the kitchen ceiling.

Week 7

- Prepped the cabinets, windows, doors, woodwork, and trim in the kitchen by filling in holes and cracks with interior spackling compound and letting it dry.
- Sanded the first application of spackling compound on the cabinets, windows, doors, woodwork, and trim and made a second application.
- Sanded the second coat of spackling compound on the cabinets, windows, doors, woodwork, and trim.
- Applied wallpaper sizing to the kitchen walls.
- Finished sanding the exterior of the kitchen cabinets.
- Primed the kitchen cabinets inside and out.
- Primed the kitchen windows, doors, woodwork, and trim.
- Painted the kitchen cabinets inside and out.
- Painted the kitchen windows, doors, woodwork, and trim.
- Mowed the lawn.

Week 8

- Repaired the garbage disposal.
- Hung wallpaper in the kitchen.
- Installed new cabinet hardware.
- Installed a new countertop.
- Installed a new kitchen light fixture.
- Installed a new range with vent hood.
- Installed a new refrigerator.
- Removed the wallpaper in the bathroom.
- Washed the ceiling, walls, window, door, and trim in the bathroom.

Month 3

The goal for this month was to complete the bathroom and refinish the floors on the first floor and then make preparations to begin working on the rough framing on the second floor.

Week 9

- Checked the second-floor drawings.
- Ordered lumber and materials for the attic.
- Painted the bathroom ceiling.
- Painted the bathroom walls, window, door, and trim.
- Installed new floor tiles in the bathroom.
- Installed a new vanity and faucet in bathroom.
- Replaced the receptacles with GFCI devices in the bathroom and utility room.
- Installed a new toilet in the bathroom.
- Installed a new light fixture and wall accessories in the bathroom.
- Washed the ceiling, walls, window, and door of the utility room.
- Painted the ceiling, walls, window, and door of the utility room.
- Replaced the washtub in the utility room.
- Mowed the lawn.

Week 10

- First rough-sanded, then fine-sanded, and then applied a penetrating sealer to the hardwood floors in the living room, dining room, hall, and two bedrooms.
- Installed new floor tiles in the kitchen and utility room.
- Displayed the building permit in the window.
- Protected the refinished floor in the hall leading to the attic stairs with drop cloths.
- Assembled carpentry tools and equipment on the second floor.

Week 11

- Built rough framing for the dormer front wall with windows.
- Cut into the roof and removed the sheathing, shingles, and rafters.
- Moved the front wall into position.
- Installed new roof rafters and plywood sheathing on the rafters, and enclosed the sides of the dormer.
- Put exterior fascia and trim on the dormers.
- Mowed the lawn.

Week 12

- Roofers patched the dormer into the existing roof, then reroofed the entire house.
- Built rough framing for two bedrooms, a hall, and a bathroom.
- Opened the heating ducts in the knee wall.
- Installed a subfloor on the second floor.
- Insulated the second-floor walls and ceilings.
- Roughed in new plumbing lines for the second-floor bathroom and installed a bathtub.

Month 4

The goal for this month was to complete the work in the new second-floor rooms by running the electric wiring and installing and painting the wallboard.

Week 13

- Ran electric lines to the second floor for the hall and bedroom lighting, switches, receptacles and for the bathroom lighting/fan, GFCI receptacles, and switches.
- Passed inspection of the plumbing and electrical rough-in work before installing wallboard.
- Installed wallboard panels in all rooms on the second floor.
- Mowed the lawn.

Week 14

- Applied wallboard tape and mud to the wallboard panels in all the rooms on the second floor.
- Sanded all wallboard joint seams, reapplied compound, and sanded.
- Installed doors, window trim, and baseboard in all the second-floor rooms.
- Primed and painted the ceilings and walls in the two second-floor bedrooms, hall, and bathroom.

Week 15

- Primed and painted the windows, doors, woodwork, and trim.
- Installed the doors and lock sets in the second-floor rooms.
- Installed ceiling light fixtures in the second-floor hall, two bedrooms, and bathroom.
- Installed vinyl tiles in the new second-floor bathroom.
- Installed tile in the bathtub surround.
- Mowed the lawn.

Week 16

- Installed the toilet, vanity and faucet, medicine cabinet, light-vent, and accessories in the second-floor bathroom.
- Had installers lay carpeting on the stairs, second-floor hall, and second-floor bedrooms.

- Installed miniblinds in the living room, dining room, bathrooms, and bedrooms.
- Installed a handrail in the staircase.
- Had the final inspection completed by the building inspector.

Month 5

The last month of the project involved a face-lift for the exterior of the house by painting it, adding shutters, and working on the driveway and the final cleanup projects.

Week 17

- Removed the storm windows and cleaned all windowsills and sashes on the exterior.
- Scraped and sanded the exterior of the windows and trim.
- Scraped and sanded the siding.
- Primed the new siding on the dormer.
- Spot-primed the windows and trim.
- Mowed the lawn.

Week 18

- Painted all siding and the dormer.
- Painted all the windows and trim.

Week 19

- Installed vinyl window shutters.
- Cleaned and refastened loose gutters.
- Scraped and sanded the front and back doors.
- Primed the front and back doors.
- Painted the front and back doors.
- Mowed the lawn.

Week 20

- Installed a new front storm door.
- Added new house numbers and mailbox.
- Washed the windows throughout the house.
- Edged the garden beds.
- Patched the driveway and applied driveway sealer.
- Mowed the lawn.
- Invited the real estate broker to tour the house.

Month 6

- Placed the house on the market.
- Mowed the lawn.

CHAPTER 20

TIMELINE FOR A LIVE-IN, FIX-UP, AND SELL-LATER HOUSE (365-PLUS DAYS)

This timeline outlines improvements that we made to a historic house. It was a folk Victorian that had been built in the late 1800s and was filled with charm and architectural appeal, but it was neglected and had been inappropriately modernized by previous owners. The location of the house was ideal—a tree-lined street complete with old-fashioned streetlights and other historic homes. Most of the houses in the neighborhood had been restored from the ground up, meaning that the costly foundation work and replacement of sills had been done. Our house was one of the smallest on the block, surely the poor cousin of the lovely restored homes in the neighborhood that sported updated kitchens and baths and nicely painted facades.

The house had been rental property with an out-of-town owner, so the interior needed considerable work. A previous owner had invested in a new foundation and repaired the house's sills. The interior work involved all of the rooms, so the plan was all-encompassing to bring the house back to its original charm and character.

The House

The house had a living room, dining room, large kitchen, and utility room on the first floor and three bedrooms and a bathroom upstairs. The small size and strange configuration of the bedroom adjacent to the bathroom made it more of a closet than a bedroom. The bathroom, while serviceable, occupied much too much space. The house originally did not have central heating or plumbing, and both of these conveniences had been added, probably in the early 1950s. Most of the pipes supplying the hot-water baseboard heat were visible. Outside the house, there was a wide porch across the front and a nice side porch off the kitchen. The house was sided in aluminum siding and had its original shutters.

The appeal of the house was its architectural elements: a handsome staircase with an intricate banister and spindles and fish-scale detail on the sides of the staircase, a wood-burning fireplace in the dining room, and a wood stove in the living room. Throughout the house, there were floor-to-ceiling windows with one-of-a-kind molded casings and heavy four-panel doors.

On the minus side, the second floor had crater-size cracks in the plaster walls and ceilings and painted pine floorboards in all the rooms and the staircase. Previous owners had "modernized" the living room with two hopper windows, and a 1950s-style pass-through in the dining room cut into the kitchen. The improvements required extensive restoration work throughout the house and modernization in the kitchen and bathrooms.

The Challenge

We had to carve out space for living, working, eating, and sleeping while making the improvements. Living in a construction zone requires considerable patience and stamina and certainly not an ounce of pride, because you have to ignore what visitors think when they see your living conditions. A shop vacuum on both floors is necessary for the ongoing exercise of removing dust and dirt from exposed wall studs, beams, and flooring.

Camping under duress is the closest analogy that comes to mind. You are not enjoying the great outdoors, but you are under considerable stress and uncertainty. It's not for everyone. Living in a work in progress also requires a continual outlay of energy and funds, so a long-term plan is important to give you a clear idea of what the results will be when the renovation is over.

The Plan

During the first three months of possession, we worked full-time on the house; after that, we worked on it piecemeal, scheduling the work around our writing business and other investment properties that we owned and managed.

Year 1

We hired a pest-control company to flea-bomb the house and eradicate the flea population before we moved in, then we put most of our furnishings and possessions into storage. We moved into the house with only the bare minimum of furniture needed to live, eat, and work in the house. We set up a small but working household on the first floor.

Phase 1: Demolish the Second-Floor Rooms, Landing, and Hall

The first phase included the heavy and dirty work of tearing out the plaster walls on the second floor. First we removed all the doors, window trim, and woodwork and marked them on the back so that we could reinstall them later. Then we broke up and removed all the old plaster walls and plastic plywood that covered some of them. We hired a helper with a truck to haul away the debris.

We cleaned up all the debris and plaster dust and set up bedroom furniture in the open space. We drove nails into the exposed wall studs for clothes hooks—very handy, indeed.

Phase 2: Attack the First Floor

In the dining room, we removed the wooden ledge and pass-through that opened into the kitchen and filled the hole with wallboard. We taped all the joints and then applied wallboard compound and let it dry; we repeated the process until the patched area was smooth and flush with the surface of the wall. We primed and painted the ceiling, wainscoting, doors, windows, woodwork, and trim and hung wallpaper above the wainscoting.

In the kitchen, we removed layers of old wallpaper and primed and painted the ceiling, doors, windows, woodwork, and trim. We applied sizing to the walls and then hung wallpaper. We scrubbed the kitchen cabinets inside and out and applied an oil finish to rejuvenate them. We removed layers of old flooring and hired an installer to lay a new subfloor and vinyl sheet flooring.

In the living room, we removed the hopper windows in the end wall and primed and painted the ceiling, doors, windows, woodwork, and trim. We removed the old wood stove, which was cracked, and built a new tile hearth for a new one that we had installed. We hired a floor sander to refinish the original pine floors in the living room, hall, and dining room and set up a minimum of furniture in the living room.

Phase 3: Attack the Second Floor

We redesigned the bedrooms to accommodate larger closets (the originals were not deep enough for hangers). We hired an electrician to rewire the second floor with new switches, receptacles, closet and overhead lighting, and three-way switch controls for the staircase. We installed insulation in all the exterior walls.

In an effort to create a smaller-footprint bathroom, we eliminated the claw-footed tub and shower stall in exchange for a tub/shower. We gave the tub to a friend and still have memories of sliding the heavy brute down the staircase and watching it come close to breaking through the front door. We enlarged the adjoining bedroom with space from the bathroom.

In the bathroom, we installed a tub/shower unit with a tile surround and light, toilet, vanity, and light/vent unit in the ceiling. We cut down the Corian countertop from the old bathroom to reuse it and installed a mirror over the vanity. We also installed new flooring and wallpaper.

Year 2

This year the push was to make the second floor of the house a bit more livable, which meant hanging drywall, repairing the windows, reinstalling the baseboard heating to conceal the piping, and adding storage space.

The Second Floor

We stripped multiple layers of paint from all the second-floor window woodwork, trim, and doors and then sanded all of it. We scraped and sanded all the window sashes and rebuilt the window frames. We framed out all the room and closet doorjambs.

We removed all exposed hot-water heating pipes and reinstalled them to be concealed by new wallboard. In each bedroom, we installed zone valves and thermostats. We added foldaway stairs to the attic to increase the storage area and reinforced the attic floor with sheathing tied into the rafters. In the attic, we increased the amount of loose-fill insulation.

We hired a drywall contractor to hang, tape, and sand wallboard in all the rooms on the second floor and the hall and stairway. We primed and painted all the new wallboard.

The First Floor

We hired a finish carpenter to design and build a bookcase with cabinets on each side of the wood stove. We installed new storm/screen doors at the front and rear of the house and built a custom-size screen for the porch door.

Year 3

During this year, we finished the detail work to complete the living space on the second floor, finished decorating in the living room, and had a small addition built to replace the utility room.

The Second Floor

We reinstalled the window trim and woodwork on the second floor and primed and painted it. We did the same with the old doors. We painted the staircase spindles, stair risers, and fish-scale molding and refinished the natural handrail. We hired a floor sander to sand and refinish the painted pine floorboards in the hall, landing, and stairs. We hired a carpeting installer to lay wall-to-wall carpeting in the three bedrooms.

The First Floor

We primed and painted the bookcase-cabinets in the living room. We rebuilt and painted the deck off the back porch because it was damaged and rotting in places.

The utility room off the kitchen was rotting away and sinking into the ground, and the furnace was on its last legs. We designed an addition to replace the utility room with a laundry-utility room and a three-quarter bathroom. The addition included a new furnace with storage closet and a laundry area with a closet. We hired a contractor to build the addition, install the furnace, build the walls, and rough in the bathroom plumbing. We painted the ceiling, walls, and trim in the addition and installed the new bathroom fixtures and wall accessories.

With all its improvements, the house has taken on a new personality, and today it stands proud and polished in its neighborhood of traditional homes. Inflation as well as the improvements we made have increased its value, to be sure.

Living in a house that's under renovation is an experience that's not for everyone, but it's truly amazing how quickly one forgets just how bad the conditions were. Ask anyone who has rehabbed a house while living there, and they often laugh at the fact that they've forgotten the anguish and unpleasant conditions. They're glad it's over, and most of them do not want to repeat the process. But there will always be some who admire old houses, and who relish the challenge of finding a neglected old house and restoring it to its original splendor.

CHAPTER 21

TIMELINE FOR A LIVE-IN, FIX-UP, AND RENT-LATER CONDO (365-PLUS DAYS)

This timeline is for the place we presently call home, a two-story, two-bedroom, $2^1/_2$-bath townhouse with a garage. When we first saw the unit, it was a vacated rental in good condition. Its location was in a desirable waterfront golf course resort with a community of homes and a complex of townhome units. Our unit is in a condominium complex of seven buildings, each with six units and garages. The buildings are set in a wooded area overlooking a golf course, so that owners have the advantage of scenic backyards with manicured greens and ponds without the responsibility of maintaining them. This community of permanent and vacation homes met our needs for a place to call home that we could live in, make improvements and add upgrades to, and hold onto for future use as rental property.

The Condo

From the entry on the first floor, the unit has a foyer with guest and utility closets, a large living room with a fireplace and dining area, an eat-in kitchen, a half-bath, and a den that opens onto a brick patio. The second floor features one large bedroom with a full bath in the front of the unit and a larger master bedroom and bath with a walk out to a deck. The bedrooms are separated by a hallway and landing and a laundry closet with a clothes washer and dryer.

The appeal of the unit was its large rooms, all of them featuring crown moldings, with a chair rail in the living and dining area. The first floor was wood and tile, and the stairs and upstairs were carpeted.

The Challenge

Our building was constructed in 1984 and had several previous owners, so the downside of the unit was its old systems and appliances which although operational would need to be replaced in the near future. We figured that we would make these improvements as they were needed, knowing that any improvements would make the unit that much more desirable as a rental unit when we moved. We approached redecorating in the same way, making cosmetic changes that we could enjoy while we lived there and that would enhance the property's value down the road.

The Plan

Year 1

Before moving in, we cleaned the condo from top to bottom. We had the carpeting throughout the second floor and stairway professionally shampooed and the tile and wood floors on the first floor cleaned and polished.

During the first few months we were living there, we noticed that the hot-water heater was marginal, so we replaced it with a new unit. We immediately noticed the lack of overhead lighting in the living-dining area, the den on the first floor, and in the two bedrooms upstairs. The lighting in all these rooms relied on lamps, so we had an electrician upgrade the system. In the main living area, we added eight recessed lights in the ceiling, spotlights over the fireplace mantel, and a dining-area fixture, all with dimmers, which greatly improved the livability of the space. In the den, track lighting was run to provide general lighting. Central ceiling fixtures were a nice improvement in the two bedrooms upstairs, too.

We removed the wallpaper in the kitchen and washed the walls; then we installed shelving in several closets to expand the storage capability of the house.

Year 2

Outside, we used a power washer to clean and spruce up the brick patio. We hired a mason to build a much-needed step landing leading from the sliding patio door off the den to the patio, which was difficult to navigate because of the steep step down to the ground.

The existing heat pump was on its last breath, so we hired a pro to replace it. After that major investment, we concentrated on small exterior cosmetic changes like painting the exterior coach lamps and the garage door. To add more storage space, we installed utility shelving in the garage and secured it to the walls for stability.

Work in progress: since we are living in the unit now, we are continuing to maintain the property and plan a major decorating push for the interior that will include painting and replacing the carpeting.

RESOURCES

Web Sites Worth a Visit

www.ashi.com. The American Society of Home Inspectors.

www.building-cost.net and **www.get-a-quote.net.** Develop a cost analysis of remodeling projects using their cost estimators.

www.coldwellbanker.com, www.prudential.com, www.realtor.com. National real estate brokers.

www.danburycreek.com and **www.newenglandclassic.com.** Use the design tools for wood panel walls systems at these sites.

www.diyornot.com. Find the cost of a job at the author's site.

www.easyclosets.com and **www.easytrack.com.** These online sites make it easy to design a closet that maximizes the space.

www.ebuild.com. This interactive catalog has more than 3,500 construction products manufacturers listed in a megadatabase.

www.energystar.gov. This government-sponsored program helps protect the environment through energy efficiency.

www.epa.gov. This government site has information about lead, asbestos, and mold found in houses.

www.ForSaleByOwner.com. Learn to sell your property yourself.

www.improvenet.com and **www.servicemagic.com** are lead-generation services to find a good local contractor.

www.irs.gov. Find real estate tax tips from the Internal Revenue Service.

www.Mapquest.com. Use this Web mapping service to locate property.

www.merillat.com. Use the site's kitchen design tool.

www.Mrlandlord.com. This site runs credit checks for landlords.

www.nahi.org. The National Association of Home Inspectors.

www.nkba.org. The National Kitchen and Bath Association.

www.nuance.com. Find information about the digital voice-to-text software Dragon NaturallySpeaking.

www.remodeling.hw.net. "Cost vs. Value Report 2007."

www.repairclinic.com. Learn how to diagnose appliance problems, fix them and order replacement parts.

www.rotorooter.com. Here's a good source of basic plumbing system information.

www.scotts.com. Get advice about lawn care and landscaping.

www.sherwin-williams.com. This manufacturer's site features a "Color Visualizer" to help you choose a color scheme.

www.zillow.com. Type in the address of your house and get an estimate of its worth.

INDEX

ABOUT
THE AUTHORS

Katie and Gene Hamilton rehabbed their first home in 1966 and were soon buying and rehabbing houses full-time. The authors of several home improvement and real estate books, they also write the nationally syndicated newspaper column "Do It Yourself . . . Or Not?". They are founders of HouseNet.com, one of the first home improvement sites on the Internet and AOL. They have appeared on CNN, HGTV, *Today*, *Dateline*, and several other programs.

CPSIA information can be obtained
at www.ICGtesting.com
Printed in the USA
LVHW051925130120
643463LV00017B/287/P

9 780071 544146